Lecture Notes in Computer Scienc

T0253938

Commenced Publication in 1973
Founding and Former Series Editors:
Gerhard Goos, Juris Hartmanis, and Jan van Leeuwen

Efthimios Tambouris   Ann Macintosh
Frank Bannister (Eds.)

Electronic Participation

6th IFIP WG 8.5 International Conference, ePart 2014
Dublin, Ireland, September 2-3, 2014
Proceedings

 Springer

Volume Editors

Efthimios Tambouris
University of Macedonia
Applied Informatics Department
Egnatia Street 156, 54636 Thessaloniki, Greece
E-mail: tambouris@uom.gr

Ann Macintosh
University of Leeds
Institute of Communications Studies
Leeds, LS2 9JT, UK
E-mail: a.macintosh@leeds.ac.uk

Frank Bannister
Trinity College
School of Computer Science and Statistics
Dublin 2, Ireland
E-mail: frank.bannister@tcd.ie

ISSN 0302-9743   e-ISSN 1611-3349
ISBN 978-3-662-44913-4   e-ISBN 978-3-662-44914-1
DOI 10.1007/978-3-662-44914-1
Springer Heidelberg New York Dordrecht London

Library of Congress Control Number: 2014948557

LNCS Sublibrary: SL 3 – Information Systems and Application, incl. Internet/Web and HCI

Typesetting: Camera-ready by author, data conversion by Scientific Publishing Services, Chennai, India

Printed on acid-free paper

Springer is part of Springer Science+Business Media (www.springer.com)

Preface

The annual international IFIP conference on electronic participation (ePart) aims to bring together researchers of distinct disciplines in order to present and discuss advances in eParticipation research. As the field of eParticipation is multidisciplinary in nature, ePart provides an excellent opportunity for researchers with backgrounds in different academic discipline to share and discuss current research on foundations, theories, methods, tools, and innovative applications of eParticipation. In addition, ePart provides a fruitful ground to nurture and plan future cooperation.

The 6th ePart conference was organized by members of IFIP Working Group 8.5 and was supported by a multidisciplinary Program Committee from all over the globe. As always, the conference was organized along with the International Conference on Electronic Government (EGOV). Both conferences are supported by the International Federation for Information Processing Working Group 8.5 on Information Systems in Public Administration (IFIP WG 8.5).

The IFIP ePart 2014 Call for Papers attracted a wide range of topics with 22 submissions, which included 11 accepted full research papers, 5 ongoing research papers and one workshop.

This volume includes complete research work organized in four groups as follows:

- Social media
- Review and Analysis
- Engaging citizens online
- Software platforms and evaluation

In addition, ongoing research papers and the workshop abstracts are published by IOS Press in a complementary proceedings volume. As in previous years, that volume covers paper contributions, workshop abstracts, and panel summaries from both, IFIP EGOV and IFIP ePart conferences. Edited by the chairs of both conferences, the volume once again illustrates the close links between ePart and EGOV, our sister conference focusing on eGovernment research.

All ePart submissions were blind peer reviewed by at least three reviewers from the ePart 2014 Program Committee with the assistance of additional reviewers. We would like to acknowledge their professionalism and rigor which has resulted in these high quality papers.

For the third time and as per the recommendation of the Paper Awards Committee, led by committee chair Olivier Glassey of IDHEAP, Lausanne, Switzerland, the IFIP ePart 2014 Organizing Committee granted an outstanding paper award. The winners were presented with their award in the ceremony at the conference dinner, which has become a highlight of each ePart conference. The names of the winners are available on the conference web page: http://www.epart-conference.org/.

IFIP ePart 2014 was hosted by the Trinity College Dublin which is situated in the heart of Dublin, Ireland. Trinity College Dublin was created by royal charter in 1592. There were 16,646 registered students in 2012/13 and over 100,277 alumni. Trinity College has a long history, whose ongoing traditions and enduring artifacts we were able to enjoy. The conference dinner was held in the marvellous 18th century dining hall. The welcome drinks were held in the atrium, which has a modern internal structure and is an obvious contrast to the more traditional dining hall.

We are grateful to a number of people who made IFIP ePart 2014 happen. We thank the members of the ePart 2014 Program Committee and the additional reviewers for their great efforts in reviewing the submitted papers. Frank Bannister and his team of Trinity College Dublin were major contributors who tirelessly organized and managed all details locally.

September 2014   Efthimios Tambouris
Ann Macintosh
Frank Bannister

Organization

Conference Chairs

Efthimios Tambouris — University of Macedonia, Greece
Ann Macintosh — University of Leeds, UK
Frank Bannister — Trinity College Dublin, Ireland

PhD Colloquium Chairs

Sharon Dawes — Center for Technology in Government, University at Albany, NY/USA
Björn Niehaves — ERCIS, Universität Münster, Germany

Program Committee and Reviewers

Steffen Albrecht — Karlsruhe Institute of Technology, Germany
Joachim Åström — Örebro University, Sweden
Frank Bannister — Trinity College Dublin, Ireland
Lasse Berntzen — Vestfold University College, Norway
Yannis Charalabidis — National Technical University of Athens, Greece
Soon Ae Chun — CUNY, USA
Todd R. Davies — Stanford University, USA
Anna De Liddo — KMi, Open University Milton Keynes, UK
Annelie Ekelin — Blekinge Institute of Technology, Sweden
Elsa Estevez — United Nations University - International Institute for Software Technology, Macao
Olivier Glassey — Institut de Hautes Etudes en Administration Publique, Switzerland
Dimitris Gouscos — University of Athens, Greece
Johann Höchtl — Danube University Krems, Austria
Naiyi Hsiao — National Chengchi University, Taiwan
Luiz Joia — FGV, Brazil
Nikos Karacapilidis — University of Patras, Greece
Roman Klinger — University of Bielefeld, Germany
Euripidis Loukis — University of Aegean, Greece
Rui Pedro Lourenço — INESC Coimbra, Portugal
Cristiano Maciel — Universidade Federal de Mato Grosso, Brasil
Ann Macintosh — The University of Leeds, UK
Rony Medaglia — Copenhagen Business School, Denmark
Yuri Misnikov — University of Leeds, UK

Table of Contents

Social Media

Review and Analysis

Engaging Citizens Online

Software Platforms and Evaluation

Social Media vs. Traditional Internet Use for Community Involvement: Toward Broadening Participation

Andrea Kavanaugh[1], John C. Tedesco[2], and Kumbirai Madondo[3]

[1] Virginia Tech, Computer Science Department, USA
[2] Communication Department, USA
[3] Sociology Department, USA
{kavan,tedesco,kmadondo}@vt.edu

Abstract. Education has consistently been the main predictor of political and civic engagement in offline and traditional Internet (i.e., email and web browsing) contexts in the US. Prior research suggests that the same 'more educated, extroverted, and activist' type of individuals (i.e., similar to opinion leaders) continued to be more engaged in civic affairs regardless of offline or online context. That is, the advent of Internet access and use did not fundamentally change the pattern of civic engagement in the US. With social media, however, the correlation between education and civic engagement may be less strong. Social media (e.g., social network sites like Facebook or MySpace, blogs and micro-blogs like Twitter, and photo and video sharing sites like Flickr and YouTube) are able to leverage offline social networks online to enable information and idea sharing among trusted sources about civic issues and concerns. In this paper we report findings from a 2012 survey of residents in the geographic community of Blacksburg, Virginia and environs. The main implication of our findings is that social media use for civic purposes is less strongly associated with and predicted by education and extroversion. As such, social media may represent a breakthrough in broadening community involvement.

Keywords: Digital government, community engagement, civic participation, Internet, social media.

1 Introduction

Education consistently has been the main predictor of political and civic engagement in offline and traditional Internet contexts (i.e., email and web browsing). Prior research on the use of traditional Internet for civic purposes suggests that the 'more educated, extroverted, and activist' type of individuals (i.e., opinion leaders) continued to be more engaged in civic affairs regardless of offline or online context. However, the use of social media for civic purposes may be less strongly correlated with education, as well as activism and extroversion. Social media (e.g., social network sites like Facebook or MySpace, blogs and micro-blogs like Twitter, and photo and

E. Tambouris et al. (Eds.): ePart 2014, LNCS 8654, pp. 1–12, 2014.

video sharing sites like Flickr and YouTube) are able to leverage offline social networks online to enable information and idea sharing among trusted sources about civic issues and concerns.

We report here findings from a 2012 survey of residents in the geographic community of Blacksburg, Virginia and surrounding Montgomery County in southwest Virginia. Located in the foothills of the Allegheny Mountains in Appalachia, Blacksburg and Montgomery County are home to the land grant university, Virginia Tech, and the community computer network known as the Blacksburg Electronic Village (BEV) that established Internet access for the public in this geographic area in 1993. The Blacksburg Electronic Village (BEV) was an early leader (1993-96) in community computer networking simply by making the Internet accessible and by training and supporting users, including residents, government, businesses, community groups, public schools and libraries. Since those early Internet years, though, the vast majority of Americans (79%) have adopted the Internet, as have most organizations [1]. Our findings from earlier studies of Internet effects on community involvement for Blacksburg and environs have been replicated in similar middle class US localities, including PrairieNet in Champaign-Urbana, Illinois, the Seattle Community Network in Seattle, Washington, and Three Rivers FreeNet in Pittsburgh, Pennsylvania [2]. Most US cities currently have a variety of locally oriented content online for community organizations, government, and neighborhoods [3]. Blacksburg and environs are still somewhat ahead of other communities on Internet penetration rates, but we are confident that findings from our investigation will continue to generalize to similar middle class towns and mixed rural areas. To the extent that Blacksburg is advanced in its use of social software [4] the results of our work will continue to contribute to community computing and political participation research.

2   Theoretical Background and Justification

Political participation theories, and most research findings on influences of civic and political participation, generally find that education is the main predictor of participation, albeit sometimes in association with political efficacy, information access, group membership and community attachment [15, 16, 17, 18, 19, 20, 21, 22]. Kavanaugh and colleagues modeled the influence of education, extroversion, and age (as external variables), and the influence of local group membership, staying informed, community collective efficacy and activism (as mediating variables) on the use of traditional Internet for civic purposes [23]. Well-educated, extroverted, informed activists with multiple group memberships (that is, essentially opinion leaders) become more involved in local community issues when they go online. Thus, traditional Internet has tended to reinforce the engagement of people who were already engaged.

In addition to education, as noted above, other variables that influence political participation include political efficacy, information access, group membership and community attachment. Along with extroversion, these variables describe opinion leaders, the 10-15% of any population who are early innovation adopters and informal (and sometimes formal) sources for advice and recommendations to others in their social network and beyond. While opinion leaders are political active, not all political activists are opinion leaders.

A number of studies on social networks have argued that political discussion networks play a crucial role in the democratic process because they give citizens the opportunity to engage in political talk and access to conflicting ideas [24, 25]. Some scholars have emphasized the importance of political talk as a precursor to political participation [26, 27]; although others have disputed this emphasis [28]. Since social media enable a rich type of interpersonal dialogue and deliberation among members of a social network, online political discussion networks can be wider and deeper than the networks generated by other types of discussion [25].

We have collected and analyzed household surveys for almost two decades (1993-2012) in Blacksburg and environs. Our results have showed a clear trend indicating that traditional Internet use (i.e., email and web browsing) for civic and political purposes has been predicted by education, extroversion, age (middle age), community group membership, collective efficacy and activism [19,20],[13]. These are also among the key defining characteristics of opinion leaders. Thus, traditional Internet use tends to reinforce the long established pattern of more educated and active members of a community using email and web browsing for greater political and civic participation.

The effects of Internet use for civic and political purposes include increased awareness and knowledge of issues, greater sharing of information and heterogeneity of discussion networks, and increased community involvement [19,20,21,22]. But if these effects only reinforce prior social patterns of involvement, traditional Internet services are primarily increasing the participation of previously more active members of a community. We have also found in our prior studies a slight increase in the involvement of those "slightly less politically active but still interested in the community". In this paper we report on findings comparing predictors of traditional Internet use for civic purposes with predictors of social media use for civic purposes. We find similar effects but for a broader, more diverse population due possibly to the game-changing nature of social media.

Our study is inspired by the preliminary finding by Smith and colleagues [10] that the use of social media (social network sites, blogs, micro-blogs) for civic purposes is not as strongly associated with socio-economic status (SES), measured by education and income, as traditional Internet use (e.g., email and web browsing).This is very important to our work. Another relevant finding from a study of blog readers asserts that participation in online discussion was predicted by education, but not in the direction traditionally found in research [23]. "Instead, it is those with less education who demonstrate more online expressive participation," (p. 46) in blogs. This suggests that web logs (i.e., blogs) may provide a pathway to political discussion and civic participation among those typically less politically active, the silent majority, and possibly the politically disillusioned and disengaged from conventional politics.

In our study results reported here, we expand on our prior (2005) model of the civic effects of Internet use [13] that seeks to explain the influence of exogenous and intermediating variables on respondents' self-reported level of community involvement since getting on the Internet. In this paper, we re-tested and compared this earlier model with social media use variables to assess their influence on civic engagement. We test the following hypotheses: 1) younger adults are using social media for civic purposes more than older adults; 2) social network factors, such as group membership, will be a stronger predictor of using social media for social purposes than 'staying informed' and 'activism'; and 3) the use of social media for civic purposes is less strongly correlated to education than the use of traditional Internet for civic purposes. Our empirical study should provide an important comparison with earlier studies as well as with our own prior results [24, 25, 26, 27].

The area of Blacksburg, Virginia and environs offers a rich opportunity to investigate the effects of Internet vs. social media use on community involvement. The majority (about 85%) of Blacksburg residents (population roughly 42,000 in 2010) are affiliated as faculty, staff, or students with the land grant university known as Virginia Tech. The neighboring town of Christiansburg (with a population of about 21,000) and Blacksburg lie within rural Montgomery County (population almost 95,000), governed by a Board of Supervisors that has jurisdiction over such services as the school district and public libraries, and some shared infrastructures, such as transportation and roads. While Blacksburg tends to be slightly above the national average in socio-economic status (as measured by education and income), in terms of Internet and social media penetration, the town of Christiansburg and the rest of Montgomery County are similar to national penetration rates on these measures. The study results reported here are from households throughout Montgomery County, including Blacksburg and Christiansburg.

3   Methods

We used purposeful sampling and combined several recruitment efforts in order to obtain a representative sample of the population. These include, along with the N of completed surveys: 1) a random sample of Montgomery County households (N=90); 2) a random sample of Virginia Tech undergraduate students (N=70); and 3) 200 local community organizations with public Facebook pages or websites (N=62). The representativeness of the sample was evaluated based on its similarity to 2010 Census statistics. The demographic statistics for our sample are similar to the demographics for the County.

The majority of respondents were white (93.8%), slightly higher than the census (87.6%). Blacks were the same as in the census (4.0%). There were a few areas of discrepancy, such as, overrepresentation of females (59.3%) vs the census (48.3%), and median income ($50,000+) compared to the census median income ($43,229). The higher median income for Blacksburg and Christiansburg - which were slightly overrepresented - lifted the overall average. Similarly, on Education only 6% of our respondents completed high school or less whereas the census has over a third (36.1%) for Montgomery County.

Survey questions asked respondents about their interests and activities, attitudes and psychological attributes, affiliation with community groups, traditional Internet and social media use, and demographic factors. This survey drew upon validated and reliable questions from prior studies, such as the HomeNet study [28], over a decade of our prior survey research in Blacksburg and environs [29,30,31,32] and relevant civic and community studies that incorporated questions about known indicators of social and civic participation [33,34,35,36,37], [23].

With our 2012 survey data, we tested the same exogenous, mediating variables or constructs, and dependent variable that we had tested in earlier path models (2005): (1) civic, political, and social interests and activities, (2) psychological attributes, such as extroversion, political and collective efficacy, and trust, and (3) Internet use [13], [32]. We compared the results with a new dependent variable: social media use for civic purposes. Our measures used Likert scales that captured respondent's agreement on frequency scales. We created typologies by aggregating variables linked to common constructs. In order to test for interrelationships among the variables, we generated correlation coefficients and tested each of these constructs for reliability.

For our exogenous variables we relied on theory and previous studies to select and test several demographic factors that predict community involvement and civic participation [3]. These include education, extroversion and age ($M=47.7$ years). Age and age squared are both are in the model, (although only age squared is shown). We measured extroversion with Likert-scale items of agreement regarding self-reported psychological and behavioral attributes: being talkative and outgoing (Cronbach alpha = 0.88). Our mediating variables include Staying Informed, Membership, Discussion Network, and Activism (for a detailed description of constructs please see http://diggov.vt.edu/constructs).

Dependent Variables. We created two path models to test our dependent variables: *Traditional Internet Use for Civic Purposes* and *Social Media Use for Civic Purposes*. The construct *Traditional Internet Use for Civic Purposes* was comprised of frequency scale items that ranged from never to several times a day. Items measured respondent's civic activities on the Internet. The questions asked respondents how often in the past six months had they used the internet for the following purposes: (1) to look for information on the Town of Blacksburg website; (2) to look for information on the Montgomery County website; (3) to look for information on Blacksburg Electronic Village (BEV) website; (4) to post factual information for other citizens; (5) to express an opinion in online forums or group discussions; (6) to communicate with other residents about local concerns or issues that interest you; (7) to get national or global news; and (8) to get local news. The alpha coefficient for this scale was a respectable 0.77.

To measure our second dependent variable, *Social Media Use for Civic Purposes,* we used questions adapted from a set of questions developed and used by the Pew Internet Study- *Social Media and Political Engagement* (2012). Participants responded to four questions that asked them if they used social network sites to receive community news or to be civically active in a group (liking or disliking a civic group, making comments about a group, and joining a community group). The measures used Likert scales that captured respondent's agreement on frequency scale that ranged from strongly disagree to strongly agree. The items held well together (α=0.85).

Statistical Analysis. Guided by our earlier research and our 2005 'civic effects of Internet Use' path model, we employed confirmatory structural equation modeling (SEM) using LISREL software to examine the explanatory power of the same variables and constructs with our 2012 survey data: education, extroversion, age (external variables), and membership, staying informed, discussion networks and activism (mediating variables) on the use of traditional internet (email and web browsing) for civic purposes (N=204). We also used SEM to examine the explanatory power of the same variables on the use of social media for civic purposes (N=155, SNS users only).

To determine whether the models were a good fit for the data, we compared the relative performance of tested models across several measures: (a) the Normed Fit Index (NFI), (b) the Comparative Fit Index (CFI), (c) the Root mean Square Error of Approximation (RMSEA), and (d) the ratio of the chi-squared statistics to the degrees of freedom for the model. The CFI and NFI are both used because they both show that a value between .90 and .95 is considered marginal, above .95 is good; below .90 is considered to be a poor fitting model. We also used the ratio of the chi-squared statistics to the degrees of freedom for the model and RMSEA as measures of relative fit with lower values taken as good model performance [37].

We used SPSS to perform some ANOVA, Correlation and Multiple Regression tests to predict differences in Internet use and social media use for civic purposes, by demographic variables (education and age) and the constructs of the model. We tested additional constructs in our study, such as, collective efficacy and political efficacy, but we report only those constructs and variables that were significant.

4   Results

4.1   Demographics and Use of Internet and Social Media

As noted above, demographically our survey respondents are generally representative of Blacksburg and surrounding Montgomery County (Census Report, 2010). The average education of respondents is college graduate. The overwhelming majority (92%) is white; more than half are female. Regarding use of the Internet and social media, the vast majority (95%) reported using the Internet and a slightly smaller majority said they use social media (80%). The highest percentage of heavy users of social network sites (SNS), such as Facebook and MySpace, are aged 18 to 29 years (48%), followed by 30 to 39 year olds (20%). Those aged 40 to 49 and 50 to 64 years old were about the same as 12% and 13%, respectively. Only 7% of adults aged 65 and older report using SNS. In general our respondents are similar to those of US national surveys (Pew, 2012). However, the average SNS and Twitter user in our sample is younger and more educated than the typical SNS and Twitter user in the US based on same year (2012) statistics from studies by the Pew Internet & American Life Project. This is important considering how demographic variables correlate with civic participation and Internet or social media use.

Correlations Among Key Constructs. Education was positively correlated with traditional Internet use for civic purposes ($r=0.273$, $p<0.05$), but education was *not* correlated with social media use for civic purposes (given limited space we have published the correlation matrix for all variables in our path models online at http://diggov.cs.vt.edu/files/Correlation matrix.pdf). There were small to moderate positive relationships between extroversion, local group membership, political discussion network, activism, and the use of both traditional Internet and social media for civic purposes.

Respondents who were older ($r=-0.197$, $p<0.001$), belonged to more groups ($r=-0.226$, $p<0.001$), stayed more informed ($r=-0.650$, $p<0.001$), and had higher levels of activism ($r=-0.475$, $p<0.001$) also had higher measures on political discussion network. Respondents who reported using traditional Internet for civic purposes ($r=-0.387$, $p<0.001$) were likely to have higher measures on political discussion network compared to respondents who reported using social media for civic purposes ($r=-0.290$, $p<0.001$).

Results from our ANOVA tests show that younger adults, aged 18-39 years, are more likely than adults over 40 to report that compared to traditional Internet (email and web browsing), using social media is more helpful in connecting with people like themselves in the local area ($F=10.147$, $p=.00$, $M=5.6$). Respondents aged 18-29 years ($F=3.28$, $p=.006$, $M=5.32$) report that compared to using traditional Internet, using social media is more helpful in feeling connected with a diversity of people in the local area. Younger adults aged 18-39 years are more likely to use social media for civic purposes.

Path Models: Traditional Internet vs Social Media for Involvement in Local Issues. To test for differences with the path models we developed in 2005, we tested two path models with our new survey data that compare outcome measures of traditional Internet use (Figure 1) and social media use for civic purposes (Figure 2).

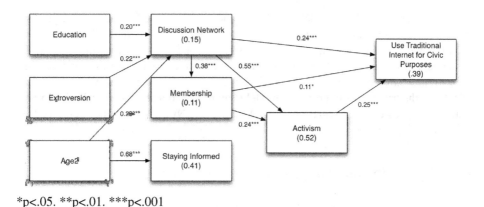

*p<.05. **p<.01. ***p<.001

Fig. 1. Model explaining Traditional Internet Use for Civic Purposes

We found that our key exogenous and mediating variables predict the use of both traditional Internet and social media for civic purposes. Education has a direct positive effect (β=.20, p<.001) on the use of both traditional Internet and social media for civic purposes. However, the indirect effect of education is greater for traditional Internet use (β=.14, p<.01) than for social media use for civic purposes (β=.09, p<.05).

Group membership is positively associated with use of traditional Internet for civic purposes (β=.11, p<.10), although the relationship is much stronger for the use of social media for civic purposes (β=.17, p<.05). A linear combination of political discussion network, membership and activism explained 39% of the variance in the use of traditional Internet for civic purposes (Figure 2); the same variables explained 26% of the variance in use of social media for civic purposes (Figure 2).

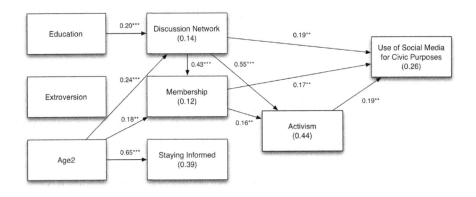

*p<.05. **p<.01. ***p<.001

Fig. 2. Model Explaining Social Media Use for Civic Purposes Model

Factor loading for both models (Figures 1 and 2) was above 0.8 indicating a strong goodness of fit. Composite reliabilities of each component were uniformly higher than 0.8 while the Cronbach alpha scores were around 0.8, thus meeting stipulated thresholds [38]. The overall fit statistics for the saturated models were good, yielding a chi-square value of 13.28 with 10 degrees of freedom (RMSEA= .04, CFI= .99, NFI = .98) for the traditional Internet use model (Figure 1) and a chi-square value of 15.86 with 12 degrees of freedom (RMSEA=.04, CFI= .99, NFI =.96) for the social media use model (Figure 2).

5   Discussion and Conclusions

The VTS project aimed to build an online "town square" to create a portal where citizens are able to learn about important local issues, identify and share local information with friends and family, and foster citizen deliberation about news and events in the community. As theoretical foundation for this paper identifies, traditional democratic theory evaluates the strength or weakness of democracies [5] by the engagement of its full range of citizens in deliberative processes and political participation behaviors. However, Dewey [10] is one of the first to explicitly articulate the need to evaluate media systems in place and whether the media characteristics foster deliberative opportunities. While this project does not aim to evaluate the quality of deliberation, it does assess use of media with different characteristics (e.g., traditional print and broadcast media, Internet, social media) and the relationships with a range of civic and political attitudes and behaviors.

Our analysis of the correlations and two path models provides a range of important insights about community members' Internet use, social media use and community involvement. We examined the strength of the relationship between education and the use of traditional Internet versus social media for civic purposes, particularly at the local level. We also analyzed new survey data in a path model that we developed earlier to try to test for differences in independent and mediating variables that explain the use of traditional Internet versus social media for civic purposes.

Our results are consistent with the preliminary 2009 Pew study finding that education is not as strongly correlated with the use of social media for civic purposes as it is with the use of traditional Internet for civic purposes. In the new path models, education has a direct positive effect on the use of both traditional Internet and social media for civic purposes. However, the indirect effect of education is greater for traditional Internet use than for social media use for civic purposes. Moreover, extroversion (outgoing and talkative), one of the defining characteristics of opinion leaders, is not significant in explaining the use of social media for civic purposes. Thus, the differences in characteristics between traditional Internet and social media appear to play an important role in fostering citizen engagement, especially by appearing to reduce the barrier related to education and seemingly engaging citizens beyond those typically identified as opinion leaders. While it is important for scholars to validate our findings in other communities and contexts, it is encouraging to report that social media extends the range and type of participant participating in civic affairs in the community.

Findings from this study appear to suggest that the communication systems, particularly features of social media, are doing a better job at serving citizens interested in engaging in civic and political affairs by engaging a broader range of citizens and reducing a significant barrier (e.g., education) to civic engagement.

Finally, political discussion network and activism, while still significant in both models, are not as strong predictors for using social media for civic purposes as they are for using traditional Internet for civic purposes. In the path model explaining social media use for civic purposes, group membership is a stronger predictor than it is for the model explaining traditional Internet use for civic purposes. These findings underscore the observation that some traditional predictors of political engagement are not as powerful in the social media environment and suggest that the social media environment broadens the characteristics of individuals engaged in civic purposes.

These findings suggest that respondents who use social media for civic purposes are not opinion leaders -- those who seemed to dominate the pattern of traditional Internet use for civic purposes. At the same time, our findings indicate the highly social nature of the civic involvement of people who use social media. Young adults (aged 18-39) are more likely than older adults to use social media for civic purposes. This is important because it shows that social media does lead to increased civic involvement especially for younger adults who traditionally have not been as involved in local issues as older adults -- a long standing trend that ended with the first Obama election in 2008.

The path models reported in this paper suggest that at least two groups typically underrepresented in civic and political processes, younger adults and those with lower education levels, are using social media to become more involved in their local communities. We encourage researchers to test the path models from this study in their local environment in the hope that the research community will learn more about ways communication tools, particularly affordances of social media, work to enlarge the access to and sharing of local information, encourage deliberation, and lead to increased citizen participation in civic and community affairs.

Acknowledgement. We are grateful for support from the National Science Foundation (SES-1111239) of which this work is part. We would also like to thank our collaborators Manuel Pérez-Quiñones, Naren Ramakrishnan and Joon Byoung Kim. Any errors, opinions, recommendations, findings or conclusions in this mateiral are those of the authors and do not necessarily reflect the views of the National Science Foundation.

References

1. Pew Internet & American Life Project. Trend Data: Internet Penetration (1995-2012) (2012), http://pewinternet.org
2. Kavanaugh, A., Schmitz, J.: Talking in lists: The consequences of computer mediated communication on communities. Internet Research Annual 1, 250–259 (2004)
3. Hampton, K.: Neighbors Online. Pew Internet & American Life Project (2010), http://pewinternet.org
4. OgilvyOne. Social Media Sells! Ogilvy & Mather (2010), http://www.ogilvy.com/News/Press-Releases/November-2010-Social-Media-Sells.aspx (retrieved November 1, 2010)
5. Almond, G.A., Verba, S.: The Civic Culture: Political attitudes and democracy in five nations. Princeton University Press, Princeton (1963)
6. Coleman, S., Blumler, J.G.: The Internet and Democratic Citizenship: Theory, practice and policy. Cambridge University Press, New York (2009)
7. Dahl, R.A.: Democracy and its Critics. Yale University Press, New Haven (1989)
8. Milbrath, L.W., Goel, M.L.: Political participation: How and why do people get involved in politics?, 2nd edn. Rand McNally College Pub. Co., Chicago (1977)
9. Norris, P.: Digital Divide: Civic engagement, information poverty, and the Internet worldwide. Cambridge University Press, New York (2001)
10. Smith, A., Verba, S., Brady, H., Schlozman, K.: The Internet and Civic Engagement. Pew Internet & American Life Project (2009), http://pewinternet.org
11. Verba, S., Nie, N.H.: Participation in America: political democracy and social equality. Harper & Row, New York (1972)

12. Verba, S., Schlozman, K., Brady, H.: Voice and Equality: Civic voluntarism in American politics. Harvard University Press, Cambridge (1995)
13. Kavanaugh, A., Carroll, J.M., Rosson, M.B., Reese, D., Zin, T.T.: Participating in Civil Society: The case of networked communities. Interacting with Computers 17, 9–33 (2005)
14. Klofstad, C., McClurg, S.D., Rolfe, M.: Measurement of political discussion networks: A comparison of two "name generator" procedures. Public Opinion Quarterly 73(3), 462–483 (2009)
15. Gonzalez-Bailon, S., Kaltenbrunner, A., Banchs, R.E.: The structure of political discussion networks: A model for the analysis of online deliberation. Journal of Information Technology 25, 230–243 (2010)
16. Jacobs, L.R., Cook, F.L., Delli Carpini, M.X.: Talking Together: Public Deliberation and Political Participation in America. University of Chicago Press, Chicago (2009)
17. Kim, J., Wyatt, R., Katz, E.: News, talk, opinion, participation: the part played by conversation in deliberative democracy. Political Communication 16(4), 361–385 (1999)
18. Schudson, M.: Why conversation is not the soul of democracy. Critical Studies in Mass Communication 14, 297–309 (1997)
19. Carroll, J.M., Reese, D.: Community collective efficacy: Structure and consequences of perceived capacities in the Blacksburg Electronic Village. In: Proceedings of the Hawaii International Conference on System Sciences (HICSS-37). IEEE Computer Society, Washinton, DC (2003)
20. Carroll, J.M., Rosson, M.B., Dunlap, D., Kavanaugh, A., Schafer, W., Snook, J.: Social and Civic Participation in a Community Network. In: Kraut, R., Brynin, M., Kiesler, S. (eds.) Domesticating Information Technologies. Oxford University Press, New York (2005)
21. Hampton, K.: Grieving for lost network: Collective action in a wired suburb. The Information Society 19(5), 417–428 (2003)
22. Kavanaugh, A.: When everyone's wired: Use of the Internet for networked communities. In: Turow, J., Kavanaugh, A. (eds.) The Wired Homestead: An MIT Press Sourcebook on the Internet and the Family, pp. 423–437. MIT Press, Cambridge (2003)
23. Zúñiga, H.G.D., Veenstra, A., Vraga, E., Shah, D.: Digital Democracy: Reimagining Pathways to Political Participation. Journal of Information Technology & Politics 7(1), 36–51 (2010)
24. Godara, J., Kavanaugh, A., Isenhour, P.: The Efficacy of Knowledge Sharing in Centralized and Self-organizing Online Communities: A Comparative Analysis of Weblogs vs Centralized Discussion Forums. In: Proceedings of the 43rd Hawaii International Conference on System Sciences (HICSS-43). IEEE Computer Society, Washington, DC (2009)
25. Kavanaugh, A., Kim, H.N., Pérez-Quiñones, M.A., Isenhour, P.: Models of local government blogging: Design trade-offs in civic engagement. In: Steinfield, C., Pentland, B., Ackerman, M., Contractor, N. (eds.) Communities and Technologies 2007, pp. 419–438. Springer, Surrey (2007)
26. Kavanaugh, A., Zin, T., Carroll, J., Schmitz, J., Pérez-Quiñones, M., Isenhour, P.: When opinion leaders blog: New forms of citizen interaction. In: Proceedings of the 7th Annual International Conference on Digital Government Research (dg.o 2006). ACM Press, New York (2006)
27. Tauro, C., Ahuja, S., Pérez-Quiñones, M.A., Kavanaugh, A., Isenhour, P.: Deliberation in the Wild: A Visualization Tool for Blog Discovery and Citizen-to-Citizen Participation. In: Proceedings of the 9th Annual International Conference on Digital Government Research (dg.o 2008). ACM Press, New York (2008)

28. Kraut, R., Kiesler, S., Bonka, B., Cummings, J., Helgeson, V., Crawford, A.: Internet paradox revisited. Journal of Social Issues 58(1), 49–74 (2002)
29. Kavanaugh, A., Patterson, S.: The impact of community computer networking on community involvement and social capital. American Behavioral Scientist 45, 496–509 (2001)
30. Kavanaugh, A., Carroll, J.M., Rosson, M.B., Zin, T.T., Reese, D.D.: Community networks: Where offline communities meet online. Journal of Computer-Mediated Communication 10(4), article 3 (2005),
    http://jcmc.indiana.edu/vol10/issue4/kavanaugh.html
31. Kavanaugh, A., Kim, B.J., Pérez-Quiñones, M., Schmitz, J.: Net gains in political participation: Secondary effects of Internet on community. Information, Communication, and Society 11(7), 933–963 (2008)
32. Kim, B.J., Kavanaugh, A., Pérez-Quiñones, M.: Toward a Model of Political Participation among Young Adults: The role of local groups and ICT use. Paper presented at the 1st International Conference on Theory and Practice of Electronic Governance, ICEGOV (2007)
33. Brady, H.: Political Participation. In: Robinson, J., Shaver, P., Wrightsman, L. (eds.) Measures of Political Attitudes. Academic Press, San Diego (1999)
34. Edwards, J., Booth, A. (eds.): Social Participation in Urban Society. Schenkman Publishing Company, Cambridge (1973)
35. Putnam, R.D.: Bowling Alone: The collapse and revival of American community. Simon & Schuster, New York (2000)
36. Shah, D., Kwak, N., Holbert, R.L.: Connecting" and Disconnecting with Civic Life: Patterns of Internet use and the production of social capital. Political Communication 18, 141–162 (2001)
37. Shah, D., Cho, J., Eveland Jr., W.P., Kwak, N.: Information and Expression a Digital Age. Communication Research 32(5), 531–565 (2005)
38. Nunnally, J., Bernstein, I.: Psychometric Theory, 3rd edn. McGraw Hill, New York (1994)

Leveraging European Union Policy Community through Advanced Exploitation of Social Media

Yannis Charalabidis[1], Euripidis Loukis[1], Yannis Koulizakis[1],
David Mekkaoui[2], and Antonis Ramfos[3]

[1] University of the Aegean, Dept. Information and Communication Systems Engineering,
Samos, Greece
{yannisx,eloukis,yanniskoul}@aegean.gr
[2] EurActiv.com, Brussels, Belgium
david.mekkaoui@euractiv.com
[3] Intrasoft International, Luxembourg
Antonis.Ramfos@intrasoft-intl.com

Abstract. The first generations of social media exploitation by government were oriented towards the general public. Evaluations of them have shown that they can provide some insights into the perceptions of the general public, however in order to achieve the required higher levels of quality, depth and elaboration it is necessary to target specific communities having strong interest and good knowledge on the particular topic under discussion. The research presented in this paper makes a contribution in this direction. It develops a novel approach to social media exploitation by the European Union (EU), which aims at leveraging its policy community, which consists of a big network of individuals/policy stakeholders having various policy related roles and capacities, geographically dispersed all over Europe. Its theoretical foundation is policy networks theory. Based on a series of workshops, in which a large number of such individuals participated, the structure of the EU policy community is initially analysed, then the proposed approach is formulated and elaborated, and finally the fuctional architecture of an ICT platform for supporting it is designed. Their main pillars are: important policy stakeholders' profiles and reputation management, relevant documents' repository and relevance rating, and finally advanced visualized presentation of them.

Keywords: Web 2.0, social media, government, policy community, policy network, reputation management.

1   Introduction

Social media have been initially exploited by private sector firms, mainly for enhancing their marketing, customer service and new products development activities, and later by government agencies, mainly for enhancing communication and interaction with citizens, increasing their engagement and participation in public policy making processes, and collecting opinions, knowledge and ideas from them, [1-5]. Though the history of social media exploitation in government is not long, there

E. Tambouris et al. (Eds.): ePart 2014, LNCS 8654, pp. 13–25, 2014.

has been a rapid evolution in the relevant practices, so that we can distinguish some discrete 'generations' in them, which are outlined in the following section 2. The first generation of social media exploitation in government was based on the manual operation of accounts in some social media, while the subsequent generations adopted more automated approaches exploiting the application programming interfaces (API) of the targeted social media [6-11]. However, all previous generations share a common characteristic: they were oriented towards the general public, and did not target any particular group. The first evaluations of them have shown that they can provide valuable insights into the perceptions of the general public, but in order to achieve the required higher levels of quality, depth and elaboration it is necessary to target specific communities having strong interest and good knowledge on the particular topic/policy under discussion [12-13].

The research presented in this paper makes a contribution in this direction. It develops a novel approach to social media exploitation by the European Union (EU), which aims at leveraging its policy community, consisting of a big network of individuals/ EU policy stakeholders having various policy related roles and capacities, and geographically dispersed all over Europe. The above context is quite interesting, due to the long and extensive debate about the EU 'democratic deficit' (see for instance [14]), one of its main dimensions being the limited accessibility of its main institutions to the multiple stakeholders of the EU policies dispersed in all member states. Its theoretical foundation is the abovementioned policy networks theory. The research presented in this paper has been conducted as part of project EU-Community (for more details see http://project.eucommunity.eu/), which has been partially funded by the 'ICT for Governance and Policy Modelling' research initiative of the EU.

The paper is organized in seven sections. In the following section 2 the background of our research is presented. Then in section 3 the research methodology is described. In the following three sections the first results of our research are outlined: the identified structure of the EU policy community (in section 4), the basic concepts of the proposed novell approach (in section 5), and the functional architecture of the required supporting ICT platform (in section 6). The final section 7 summarizes the conclusions and proposes future research directions.

2   Background

2.1   Social Media in Geovernment

It is widely accepted that social media have a good potential to drive important and highly beneficial innovations in government agencies, both in the ways they interact with the public outside their boundaries, and in their internal operations and decision making [5]. They can lead to the creation of new models and paradigms in the public sector: i) social media-based citizen engagement models, ii) social media-based data generation and sharing models, and iii) social-media based collaborative government models [3]. According to Don Tapscott [15] 'the static, publish-and browse Internet is being eclipsed by a new participatory Web that provides a powerful platform for the reinvention of governmental structures, public services and democratic processes', leading to the emergence of a new 'Government 2.0' paradigm, which is quite different from the previous paradigms. Social media provide to government agencies big opportunities for: i) increasing citizens' participation and engagement in public policy making, by providing to more groups a voice in discussions of policy development, implementation and evaluation; ii) promoting transparency and accountability, and in this way reducing corruption, by enabling governments to open up large quantities of activity and spending related data, and at the same time enabling citizens to collectively take part in monitoring the activities of their governments; iii) crowdsourcing solutions and innovations, by exploiting public knowledge and creativity in order to develop innovative solutions to the increasingly complex societal problems [1-5].

The first generation of social media exploitation in government was based on the manual operation of accounts in some social media, posting relevant content to them (e.g. concerning current and future policies and activities) manually, and then reading citizens' interactions with it in order to draw conclusions from them. It was quickly realized that this approach was inefficient, and this gave rise to the development of a second generation of social media exploitation in government, which is characterised by higher level of automation of the above tasks, taking advantage of the extensive and continuously evolving API that social media increasingly provide [6-8]. In particular, the main characteristics of this second generation are:

a) the automated posting of policy related content in multiple accounts of the government agency in various social media, using their API, in order to stimulate citizens' reactions and relevant discussion,

b) the automated retrieval of various types of citizens' interactions with this content (such as number of views, likes and retransmissions, comments, etc.), and/or other relevant content, using again the corresponding API,

c) and the sophisticated processing of these interactions in order to support drawing conclusions from them.

This approach can be viewed as an 'active crowdsourcing' by government, in which the latter poses a specific policy related topic/question through its postings, and aims to collect citizens' reactions, proposals and ideas on it.

However, the above approach necessitates that citizens are attracted in the social media accounts of government agencies, and move their political discussion there. Very often this is difficult: citizens have already some well established electronic spaces where they are conducting their political discussions, such as various political blogs, news sites, etc., which they perceive as more 'independent' and friendly, and they find no reason to move their political discussions to government agencies' social media accounts. This gave rise to the development of a third generation of social media exploitation by government [9-11], in which government agencies go beyond their social media accounts:

i) they retrieve the extensive public policy related content created by citizens freely (without any government initiation, stimulation or moderation) in numerous social media sources (e.g. political blogs and microblogs, news sites, etc.), in a fully automated manner, using their API,

ii) and make advanced linguistic processing of it, in order to extract needs, issues, opinions, proposals and arguments raised by citizens on a particular domain of government activity or policy of interest.

This extension can be viewed as 'passive crowdsourcing' by government, in which the latter is not actively conducting crowdsourcing (by posing to citizens particular discussion topics or questions, as in the previous approach), but remains passive, just 'listening' to what citizens discuss, and analyzing the content they freely produce.

The above three generations of social media exploitation by government share a common characteristic: they were oriented towards the general public, and did not target any particular group. The first evaluations of them (e.g. [7], [12-13]) have shown that they can provide useful 'high-level' information concerning advantages and disadvantages of existing government policies, and also important issues and problems, as perceived by social actors, as well as some solution directions they propose. This information is definitely useful for the design of public policies taking into account the perceptions and opinions of the general public. However very often it is at a too high level and lack depth and elaboration. Therefore in order to achieve more depth, elaboration and quality it is necessary to target specific communities that have strong interest and good knowledge on the particular topic/policy under discussion. In this direction policy networks can be very useful; in the following section a review of previous literature on them is provided.

2.2   Policy Networks

Extensive research has been conducted in the political sciences concerning policy networks, which has revealed their importance in the modern governance system for the formulation and implementation of public policies [16 - 18]. As policy networks are defined sets of formal and informal institutional linkages between various both governmental actors and non-government actors (such as representattives of professions, labour unions, big businesses and other interest groups) structured around shared interests in public policy-making and implementation. They first gained currency and importance in the 1970s and especially the 1980s, when governments expanded their involvement in society and the economy, so policy making became much more complex, specialized, and fragmented than previously. In this context of increased complexity and specialization governments realised that previous unilateral modes of governance are insufficient, since they needed the resources and cooperation of non-state actors (initially economic actors and later other social actors as well) in order to have predictability and stability in their policy-making environments. The emergence of policy networks, in which state actors and non-state actors were cooperating (and sometimemes bargaining) for policy formulation and implementation was seen as a response to this context. This trend was strengthened later due to the increasing complexity of the big social problems that had to be addressed through public policies, the globalisation of the economy, and also the emergence of supranational governance institutions, such as the European Union, which undertook some competences from national governments, reducing their power and intervention capacity [19-21]. In policy networks the non-state actors provide to the state actors on one hand information, knowledge and expertise, and on the other hand support for the formulation and implementation of public policies, and legitimization of them; in return the former have the opportunity to influence the public policies (e.g. legislation, allocation of government resources) towards directions beneficial to them.

There are important differences among policy networks functioning in various countries and sectors with respect to several characteristics, such as the number and type of participants, the balance of power among them, the distibution of important resources, the density of interaction among participants, the degree of homogeneity in value and beliefs and the functions performed, which impact significantly participants' behaviour and policy outcomes [22-25]. This has lead to the development of several policy network typologies. In [22-23] eight types of policy networks are identified, based on three structural characteristics of the participating state and society actors: the bureaucratic autonomy and the coordination capacity of the state actors, and the degree of mobilization and organizational development/capacity of societal actors; each of them is more appropriate for a particular context (sector type:expanding, stabilizing or declining) and policy type: anticipatory, or reactive)). It should be noted that in some of these policy networks government agencies are dominant (state directed networks), in some others societal actors have more power (clientele pluralist networks), while there are more 'balanced' ones in which there is balance of power between state and economic actors (corporatist networks). Another important characteristic of policy networks is the density of interactions among participants: according to [25] networks that are stable over time and are characterized by dense interactions among network members can foster the development of shared values and beliefs concerning desirable policy objectives and instruments, and also cooperation rules.

At the same time policy networks are important mechanisms for and facilitators of policy changes in cases of important changes in the external context (e.g. economic, ideological, knowledge, institutional changes) [25-27]. Contextual changes are sensed by one or more network's actors, who inject new ideas to the network, which are then transmitted to the other actors; furthermore, very often external context changes lead to changes in policy network's composition, entry of new actors, and also changes in the levels of influence of the existing actors. The above lead to collective awarenes of the changing external context and the inability of network to address it, and to changes of the perceived strategic interests of the individual network partners and the balance of strategic resources among them, resulting in the gradual development of new foundations and bases for collective strategic action, and finally incremental or paradigmatic policy changes.

Policy networks today play in general a significant role in deciding which issues will be included and excluded from the policy agenda, in shaping definitions of policy problems, and also the behaviour of actors through defining 'the rules of the game', in the selection of appropriate solutions, privileging certain interests and in general in shaping the substance of public policy [18]. For this reason it is important that policy networks are 'balanced' (=include all the important stakeholders) and transparent (=the positions of the stakeholders are visible and clear, and serve as bases for the formulation of public policy) to the highest possible degree.

3   Research Methodology

In order to gain a better understanding of the structure of EU policy community, formulate and elaborate the proposed approach of leveraging it by exploiting the social
media, and also collect the specific users' requirements from a supporting ICT platform, thirteen workshops (named as CreActiv1 to Creactiv13) were organized as part
of the preparation and the implementation of the abovementioned EU-Community
project. The EurActiv.Com (a leading EU policy online media network
(www.euractiv.com), which participates as partner in this project) and the Fondation
EurActiv Politech (a public service foundation (www.euractiv.com/fondation) having
as main mission 'to bring together individuals and organisations seeking to shape
European Union policies, also partner of this project') were the organizers of these
workshops. The participants were various representatives of important EU policy
stakeholders (such as industry federations), members of the advisory boards of Eu-
rActiv.Com and Fondation EurActiv Politech, thematic experts in several EU policies
(such as the renewable energy policies), policy analysts, registered users of EurAc-
tiv.Com portals; also permanent staff of various hierarchical levels from the European
Commission, including the Director-General of European Commission DG Connect.

The first five workshops aimed mainly to gain a better understanding of the structure of EU policy community, and also to formulate and elaborate the proposed approach. The next five workshops had as main objective to elicit and collect users'
requirements from an ICT platform suppoting the implementation of this approach.
The final three workshops aimed to validate and elaborate the findings of the previous
ones; also their participants filled a questionnaire concerning the EU policy related
tasks they needed support for. The large experience of EurActiv.Com and Fondation
EurActiv Politech in EU public policies formulation through extensive consultation
with stakeholders (who very often publish stakeholders' position documents on various EU thematic policies in the portals of EurActiv.Com) was very useful for the
successful execution of the above tasks.

4   Structure of EU Policy Community

From our analysis it has been concluded that the EU, due to the big number of its
involvement and intervention domains, the complexity and at the same time the
importance of its policies, which concern its 27 member states (being quite heterogeneous in terms of economic development, political traditions, culture, etc.), has a large
policy community. There are numerous social groups, organizations and persons, both
in Brussels and in the 27 member states' capitals, who have some interest in EU policies and make systematically contributions in order to influence them (e.g. express
opinions, positions and proposals, or provide relevant information and expertise). The
EU relies much on these contributions. The above EU policy community can be
broadly divided into three groups:

I) <u>Decision makers:</u> This group includes mainly the 'institutional triangle' formed
by the Commission, representing the general interests of the EU, the European

Parliament, representing the peoples, and the Council, representing the Member States; these three institutions lay down the policies and legislative acts that apply throughout the EU. It also includes the European Investment Bank, the European External Action Service and the decenrtalised agencies and bodies (currently they are about 30). There are numerous employees of the above organizations involved in the formulation and implementation of EU policies with various roles.

II) Influencers: This group includes several hundred EU industry federations representing the interests of their industries at European level, and also many 'think tanks', mainly policy or research institutes performing research and advocacy concerning various EU policy related topics, such as social policy, technology, economic policy and culture; most of them are non-profit organizations, funded by governments, parties, advocacy groups, or businesses, or derive revenue from consulting or research work related to their projects. Furthermore this group includes many non-governmental organizations (NGOs), which pursue various social aims, operating independently from any form of government. Finally there are many multinational corporations having offices in Brussels, which aim to represent and promote their interests and requirements concerning their activities in the European market.

III) Policy Analysts: This group includes many international media organisations that have journalists specialised and highly knowledgeable in EU policies and operation (some of these media are generic, while some others specialised in the EU, such as the EurActiv.Com). Also, there are many Brussels-based consultancy firms, which have expertise in the EU policy process in general, or in particular policy domains, and provide companies, public and private institutions, with guidance and support for influencing EU policies and decisions and having access to European funds.

5   The Proposed Approach

Based on the conclusions of the evaluations of previous generations pf social media exploitation in government (section 2.1), on the previous research on policy networks (section 2.2), and also on the analysis of the needs of the EU policy stakeholders (using the research methodology described in section 3), we developed a novel approach to social media exploitation by government agencies that aims at leveraging their policy networks. It focuses on leveraging the extensive policy community of the EU (which has been described in the previous section 4) through advanced exploitation of social media, however it has a wider applicability for any type of government agency. From our workshops (see section 3) a clear conclusion was that the main need of EU policy stakeholders is to be better informed on the most knowledgeable and credible people and the most relevant documents on a specific policy related topic they are interested in, and also to associate the latter with the stages of the EU policy processes.

Therefore the main characteristics of the proposed approach are:
- it focuses on the EU policy community, and not on the general public, and aims to leverage it by increasing its 'interaction density' and also interaction quality, which as

mentioned previously in section 2.2 fosters the development of shared values and beliefs concerning desirable policy objectives and instruments ([16], [25]), and finally to increase the efficiency and effectiveness of this community;

- it provides support not only to the EU decision makers on policy formulation and implementation issues, but also to the other groups of the EU policy community as well, such as the various types of influencers and policy analysts, in order to exchange information, knowledge and expertise, and also opinions, positions and proposals, and improve their capacity to participate in and contribute to the EU policy processes,

- it adopts a 'selective' approach, focusing on the most knowledgeable and credible people on each topic we are interested in, by using advanced reputation management methods [28] (see following section 6 for more details),

- and also focusing on the most relevant documents (such as web pages, blog posts, social media content, online comments, word/pdf documents, collected from various external sources) on each topic we are interested in, using documents' curation/relevance assessment methods (see following section 6 for more details).

An overview of our approach is shown below in Figure 1.

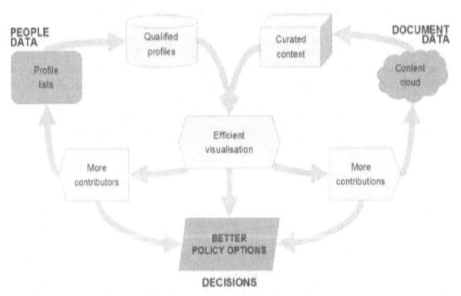

Fig. 1. Overview of the proposed approach to social media exploitation by government agencies for leveraging their policy networks

We remark that it consists of three main processes: the first two of them crawl at regular time intervals the most relevant external sources of EU policies knowledgeable and credible people, and also of relevant documents of various types, update the corresponding databases, and also assess their reputation/credibility of the former and the relevance of the latter. These databases are used by the third process, which processes users' queries (e.g. concerning the most reputable/credible people or the most relevant documents on a specific topic) and presents the results, making use of visualisation/visual analytics techniques [29].

6   ICT Platform Architecture

An ICT platform has been designed for supporting the implementation of the above approach, and its architecture is shown in Figure 2. It consists of three components, named as EurActory, CurActory and PolicyLine, which correspond to the abovementioned three main processes.

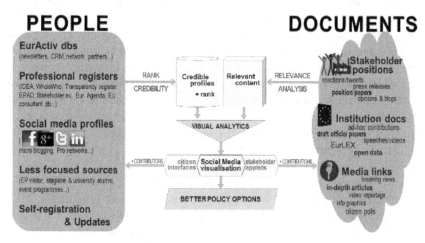

Fig. 2. ICT Platform Architecture

The first 'EurActory' component crawls at regular time intervals various external sources of profiles of people with high levels of knowledge, expertise and credibility in one or more EU policies, such as the databases of EurActiv.Com, various professional registers, social media profiles, etc., and updates the corresponding EurActory EU policies knowledgeable and credible people database; also, the capability of self-registration of people who believe that they have good knowledge of one or more EU policies is provided as well. Furthermore this component will perform credibility ranking, based on the following criteria (each of them having a specific weight):

- Self-evaluation: direct user input.
- Peers rating: based on a survey sent to most influencial users.
- Participation as speaker in important events on EU policies: through events' programs uploading, and speakers' names recognized and credited
- Organisation reputation: google ranking of the organisation name
- Position ranking (e.g. see EC Org Charts IDEA): based on scale of hierarchy
- Document assessment: results of authored documents' assessment by their readers
- Proximity trust: level of connection in social media
- Past reputation levels: taking into account reputation in previous months (its stability means credibility).

The second 'CurActory' component crawls at regular time intervals various external sources of documents related to EU policies, such as websites of EU institutions (e.g. European Commission), relevant media (such as EurActiv, European Voice, EU Observer) and various EU policy stakeholders, and also social media accounts where relevant posistions and opinions are published, and updates the corresponding CurActory documents database. Also, the capability of manuall adding a document relevant to an EU policy/subpolicy is provided as well. These documents (with the widest meaning of this term including web pages, blog posts, social media content, online comments, word/pdf documents, etc.) are first related to the most relevant policy topic and subtopics (one document may match more than one subtopic), and then linked to one or more authors in the EurActory people database. Next, for each document its relevance is rated with respect to the above policy topic/subtopic (as one document may match more than one subtopic, it may as well get more than one rating, depending on the subtopic it is considered for). The criteria for this relevance assessent are:

- Author: his/her credibility ranking for the sepcific topic/subtopic.
- Social Media: is it engaging on social media?
- Quality: is it accurate? Or even valuable?
- Relevance: is it relevant to the topic? Or even timely?
- Endorsement: do you agree on the issues? Or even the solutions proposed?

(the last three criteria are rated by the readers, in a rating pop up window).

The third 'PolicyLine' component using the databases of the other two components enables a user to enter a specific policy related topic/subtopic and search for i) people with high levels of knowledge and credibility on it - the result will be the top ones in credibility ranking - or ii) for relevant documents – the result will be the documents with the highest relevance assessent in a PolicyLine visualisation form, which is shown in Figure 3, and includes four columns:

a) In the first column from the right it is shown in which of the steps of EU policy process (public debate, policy debate, draft, debate, decision, implementation, review) the particular topic/subtopic is

b) In the central column (seconfd from the left) there are links to various categories of official relevant documents from EU Institutions (e.g. white papers, green papers, Commission drafts, amendments, etc.)

c) In the first column from the left there are links to various stakeholder positions documents (e.g. from industry federations, NGOs, etc) related to the relevant official documents)

d) In the second column from the right there are links to relevant media analysis documents from EurActiv and other media, which are related to the relevant official documents.

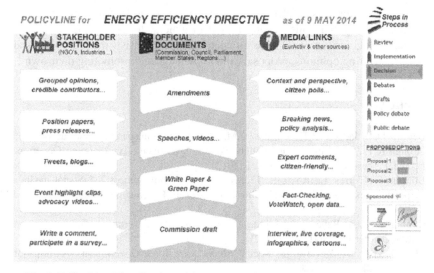

Fig. 3. PolicyLine Visualisation of documents relevant to a specific topic/subtopic

7   Conclusions

The first generations of social media exploitation in government were oriented mainly towards the general public, aiming to increase and enhance communication with them concerning various public policies under formulation or implementation. The research presented in the previous sections of this paper aims to develop a novel approach to social media exploitation in government, which is oriented towards leveraging the policy networks (consisting of various government and non-government actors having high levels of interest in and knowledge and experience on particular topics/policies). Its theoretical foundation is the policy networks theory, which has been developed through extensive political sciences research that has been conducted in this area (briefly outlined in 2.2). This novell approach can give rise to a new fourth generation of social media exploitation in government, which is more focused on highly know-ledgeable policy communities and networks. It does not aim to replace the previous wide public oriented generations (this would be negative for our democracy), but to co-exist and be combined with them. There should be a balanced development of both these two orientations of social media use in government (towards the wide public and the policy networks respectively), and a complementarity between them: it is equally important for government agencies on one hand to gain insights into the feel-ings and perceptions of the citizens, and on the other hand to collect information, expertise, proposals and opinions from highly knowledgeable policy networks.

Further research is in progress as part of this project, which is going to evaluate the proposed approach in several pilot applications. This will allow us to assess the value of this approach along the main questions/dimensions proposed by policy networks theory (see section 2): To what extent it assists the EU institutions in collecting high quality opinions, proposals and knowledge from their policy networks? To what extent it is useful for sensing changes in their external context, for designing and implementing the required policy changes, and in general for increasing the dynamic capabilities of EU institutions ? Also, to what extent it is assists the EU policy stakeholders in collecting opinions, proposals and knowledge and promoting their own ?

References

1. Bertot, J.C., Jaeger, P.T., Grimes, J.M.: Promoting transparency and accountability through ICTs, social media, and collaborative e-government. Transforming Government: People, Processand Policy 6(1), 78–91 (2012)
2. Bonsón, E., Torres, L., Royo, S., Flores, F.: Local e-government 2.0: Social media and corporate transparency in municipalities. Government Information Quarterly 29, 123–132 (2012)
3. Chun, S.A., Luna Reyes, L.F.: Editorial - Social media in government. Government Information Quarterly 29, 441–445 (2012)
4. Margo, M.J.: A Review of Social Media Use in E-Government. Administrative Sciences 2(2), 148–161 (2012)
5. Criado, J.I., Sandoval-Almazan, R., Gil-Garcia, J.R.: Government innovation through social media. Government Information Quarterly 30, 319–326 (2013)
6. Charalabidis, Y., Loukis, E.: Participative Public Policy Making Through Multiple Social Media Platforms Utilization. International Journal of Electronic Government Research 8(3), 78–97 (2012)
7. Ferro, E., Loukis, E., Charalabidis, Y., Osella, M.: Policy Making 2.0: From Theory to Practice. Government Information Quarterly 30(4), 359–368 (2013)
8. Ferro, E., Loukis, E., Charalabidis, Y., Osella, M.: Analyzing the Centralised Use of Multiple Social Media by Government from Innovations Diffusion Theory Perspective. In: Wimmer, M.A., Tambouris, E., Macintosh, A. (eds.) ePart 2013. LNCS, vol. 8075, pp. 95–108. Springer, Heidelberg (2013)
9. Wandhöfer, T., Taylor, S., Alani, H., Joshi, S., Sizov, S., Walland, P., Thamm, M., Bleier, A., Mutschke, P.: Engaging Politicians with Citizens on Social Networking Sites: The WeGov Toolbox. International Journal of Electronic Government Research 8(3), 22–43 (2012)
10. Bekkers, V., Edwards, A., de Kool, D.: Social media monitoring: Responsive governance in the shadow of surveillance? Government Information Quarterly 30(4), 335–342 (2013)
11. Charalabidis, Y., Loukis, E., Androutsopoulou, A., Karkaletsis, V., Triantafillou, A.: Passive Crowdsourcing in Government Using Social Media. Transforming Government: People, Process and Policy 8(2) (2014)
12. Loukis, E., Charalabidis, Y., Androutsopoulou, A.: An Analysis of Multiple Social Media Consultations in the European Parliament from a Public Policy Persepctive. In: European Conference on Information Systems (ECIS), Tel Aviv, Israel (2014)
13. Xenakis, A., Androutsopoulou, A., Koutras, C., Charalabidis, Y., Loukis, E.: Description of the NOMAD Evaluation Methodology – Deliverable 7.3 (2014)
14. Chryssochoou, D.: Democracy and the European polity. In: Cini, M. (ed.) European Union Politics, 2nd edn., Oxford University Press, Oxford (2007)
15. Tapscott, D.: Government 2.0: Rethinking Government and Democracy for the Digital Age. In: Gøtze, J., Pedersen, C.B. (eds.) State of the eUnion - Government 2.0 and Onwards. AuthorHouse, Copenhagen (2009)

16. Skogstad, G.: Policy Networks and Policy Communities: Conceptual Evolution and Governing Realities. In: Workshop on "Canada's Contribution to Comparative Theorizing" Annual Meeting of the Canadian Political Science Association, University of Western Ontario, London, Ontario (2005)
17. Rhodes, R.A.W.: Policy Network Analysis. In: Moran, M., Rein, M., Goodin, R.E. (eds.) The Oxford Handbook of Public Policy, pp. 423–445. Oxford University Press, Oxford (2006)
18. Rhodes, R.A.W.: Understanding Governance: Ten Years On. Organization Studies 28(8), 1243–1264 (2007)
19. Pfetsch, F.R.: Negotiating the European Union: A Negotiation-Network Approach. International Negotiation 3, 293–317 (1998)
20. Ansell, C.: The Networked Polity: Regional Development in Western Europe. Governance 13(3), 303–333 (2000)
21. Peterson, J.: The choice for EU theorists: Establishing a common framework for analysis. European Journal of Political Research 39, 289–318 (2001)
22. Atkinson, M., Coleman, W.: Strong States and Weak States: Sectoral Policy Networks in Advanced Capitalist Economies. British Journal of Political Science 19, 47–67 (1989)
23. Coleman, W., Skogstad, G. (eds.): Policy Communities and Public Policy in Canada. Copp Clark Pitman, Toronto (1990)
24. Van Waarden, F.: Dimensions and types of policy networks. European Journal of Political Research 21, 29–52 (1992)
25. Marsh, D., Smith, M.: Understanding Policy Networks: towards a Dialectical Approach. Political Studies 48, 4–21 (2000)
26. Howlett, M.: Do Networks Matter? Linking Policy Network Structure to Policy Outcome: Evidence from Four Canadian Policy Sectors 1990-2000. Canadian Journal of Political Science 35(2), 235–267 (2002)
27. Atkinson, M.M., William, D.: Policy Networks, Policy Communities and the Problems of Governance. Governance 5(2), 154–180 (1992)
28. Li, H., Benyoucef, M., Bochmann, G.V.: Towards a global online reputation. In: The Proceedings of the International Conference on Management of Emergent Digital EcoSystems (2009)
29. Keim, D.A., Kohlhammer, J., Ellis, G.P., Mansmann, F.: Mastering The Information Age – Solving Problems with Visual Analytics. Eurographics, Germany (2010)

Genres of Participation in Social Networking Systems: A Study of the 2013 Norwegian Parliamentary Election

Marius Rohde Johannessen

Buskerud and Vestfold University College, Department of Business and Management
P.O. Box 235, 3603 Kongsberg, Norway
marius.johannessen@hbv.no

Abstract. Online campaigning has been on the agenda of Norwegian political parties since 2001. In 2007, there were some early attempts at online campaigning through social networking systems (SNS) during the municipal elections. 2009 was the first time SNS' were used for campaigning on a national level by all the political parties represented in parliament. This study follows up an earlier study of the 2009 election by examining the communication genres being used by Norwegian political parties in the 2013 parliamentary election. The 2009 study concluded that a genre system for online campaigning was emerging in SNS', and presented an overview of this system. This paper shows that the genre system is slowly moving towards an established system, and that while still not fully sorted out, previous issues, such as a lack of two-way communication, is being addressed by the parties. The study concludes that campaigning in SNS' is slowly moving more and more towards the objectives of politics 2.0.

Keywords: eParticipation, online campaigning, social networking systems, genre theory, Norway.

1 Introduction

Online campaigning has been on the agenda for Norwegian political parties since the parliamentary election in 2001. Back then the Internet played a marginal role, but it was expected that this would change in coming election campaigns [1]. In 2007 there were some initial attempts at campaigning through social media, and Barack Obama's successful 2008 campaign served as an inspiration for the 2009 parliamentary election [2].

The reason for this interest in moving towards digital media can be found in the Norwegian research project power and democracy, which conducted a study of the state of democracy in Norway between 1998 and 2003. One of the main conclusions of the study was that representative democracy is in decline. Citizens are no longer loyal to one political party, or participating in broad social movements such as labour unions. Citizens instead move from one party to the next, one issue to the other. Single issues have become more important than party politics. This means that power is slowly moving from the parliament towards lobbying and non-governmental organi-

E. Tambouris et al. (Eds.): ePart 2014, LNCS 8654, pp. 26–37, 2014.

zations (NGO's) [3]. Norwegian politicians are signalling that they want more citizen dialogue and user-involvement in the political process [4], and they are increasingly attempting to achieve this through SNS' and other digital communication channels in order to reach out and communicate directly with voters [5]. The purpose of this paper is to revisit the SNS communicative strategies of Norwegian political parties. In the 2009 parliamentary election there was evidence of an emerging system of genres [6] for political communication, and the political parties reported that their SNS efforts would only increase with time. This paper thus aims to compare the findings from the elections in 2009 and 2013, in order to examine if the genre system emerging in 2009 has changed significantly between the two elections, and to discover if SNS' are being used in line with the principles of online politics as outlined by Chadwick and Howard [7].

The rest of the paper is structured as follows: Section two provides an overview of related research, specifically on the topics of social networking and online campaigning. Section three presents the research approach of the study, and sections four and five present the findings and conclusions with some possible directions for future research.

2   Related Research

Democracy can be conceptualized in a number of ways, and is practiced differently in different contexts [8]. Most of these conceptualisations involve some sort of interaction between citizens and government. Communication between citizens and the politicians elected to rule is considered a necessity in the democratic process, and government generally recognise the value of participation [9, 10] . While the value of citizen participation is recognized both in academia and government, recent political trends show that political engagement is decreasing. Across the western world fewer people are members of a political party [11] or vote in elections [12]. Governments rely more on expert assessment [13] and power moves towards markets and the legal system [14]. Partly as a consequence of this, the past decade has seen a number of technologically driven participation projects, as there are indications that social media presence increases participation [15].

2.1   Online Campaigning in SNS: Towards Politics 2.0

Social Networking Services (SNS') are web-based services where users can 1) create and maintain a public or private profile. 2) create a list of other users they are connected to, and 3) see their own and others' contact lists [16]. The most popular SNSs are those that focus on user-generated content, participation, openness and network effects [17]. Social networking is not mainly about technology, but about covering people's needs for access to and sharing of information, collaboration and the creation of identity and self. As such, SNS should be treated more as a cultural than technological phenomenon [18]. To reap the benefits of SNS, owners of information needs to open their data, think in terms of collaborative production of ideas and content, and to share ideas with others in order to create better information[19].

Political campaigning is all about convincing the public that your party has the best policy. The election campaign has a very big influence on the outcome of the parliamentary election. More than 40 % of Norwegian voters wait until the final weeks of the campaign before deciding who gets their vote, and many change their mind several times during the campaign [20]. Younger voters are more likely to cast their vote differently from one election to the next [21]. When the Norwegian newspapers became politically independent, political parties lost the power to decide what should be on the public agenda [3]. The media has taken over this role, and are trying to write about the things they believe voters are concerned about [3, 21]. Political parties in campaign mode are constantly working to move citizens towards those media channels controlled by the parties, where SNS' along with party and candidate web sites are among the most important [5]. SNS' play an important part in what has been called the *hybridised media system*, where traditional and new media are both reliant upon each other [22], and thus SNS' expand the possible modes of election campaigning [23].

Chadwick and Howard [7] introduce the concept of politics 2.0, based on the original conceptualisation of web 2.0 made by O'Reilly [24]. This concept can be used for analysing the media-specific effects of campaigning in SNS', and can function as a guideline for practitioners and as a lens for understanding and evaluating SNS activities. The concept consists of up of 7 themes: 1) *The Internet is a platform for political discourse* where the ability to rapidly respond to events through setting up new web sites or SNS groups is essential. Distributed networks of contributors, online activist campaigns and citizen journalism can create valuable information, which leads to the second theme: 2) *The collective intelligence emergent from political web use.* 3) *The importance of data over particular software and hardware applications* is a theme showing that not only does SNS' provide rich input from citizens, but it is also a source of demographic data about potential voters. 4) *Perpetual experimentalism in the public domain.* This theme shows how SNS' can contribute to more inclusive politics, by taken citizen advice into consideration and by providing a platform where political parties can instantly respond to comments, polls, petitions and media events. 5) *The creation of small scale forms of political engagement.* Data mash-ups such as fix my street, as well as mobile applications where citizens produce data through mobile apps or through documenting issues using mobile cameras allows for low-threshold forms of engagement. This is tied in with the sixth theme 6) *The propagation of political content over multiple applications.* Finally, the seventh theme includes the new interactive features found in SNS' such as multimedia content and hyperlinks: 7) Rich *user experiences on political web sites.* The importance and potential outcomes of interactive content have been discussed in several earlier studies [25-27].

2.2   Genre Theory

Genre theory can be applied to study the role of communication in social processes, and has been applied to several eParticipation studies [28-31]. Genres evolve over time, in the interplay between institutional practice and the people communicating [32]. Genre theory provides us with a lens for detailed understanding of political communication, beyond the observation of technological functionality [33]. Originally, genres were recognized by having similar form and content, where form refers to physical and linguistic features, and content to themes and topics of the genre [32]. Later, when the Internet became more popular, functionality offered by the medium delivering the genre was added as a third construct [26]. A set of genres used by a given community can be seen as a genre system [6] The genre system of a community can reveal a "rich and varied array of communicative practices" shaped by community members in response to norms, events, time pressure and media capabilities [33]. Genres are useful for studying SNS', as the introduction of new media over time often leads to new communication practices which genre theory allows us to map and analyze [30]. By studying communication genres instead of the technology used to communicate, we can discover how communication changes and evolves over time [33], and by including the technological functionality of the medium the genre is enacted within, we can better understand the interplay between the social and the technical [26].

Genres can be defined by examining form, functionality and content, by using the 5w1h-method By asking *where, why, when, who, what* and *how*, we can uncover the purpose, contents, placement in time, location, participants, structure and medium for communication [6, 34]: *Where* tells us where the communication takes place, the medium being used, or the physical location. *Why* explains the purpose of the genre, as understood by those using it. *When* refers to the time where communication takes place. For example, the "job application" genre is enacted when applying for a job, and needs to be in by a set date. *Who* defines the actors involved in communication, the sender and receiver of the genre. *What* is the content of the genre, and defines what is being communicated, and any relations to other genres. Finally, *How* describes the technical needs for delivery of the genre, for example which medium is being used, or any other technical necessities.

3   Research Approach

The objective of this paper is to examine if the genre system emerging in 2009 has changed significantly between 2009 and 2013, and to discover if SNS' are being used in line with the principles of politics 2.0. The study was conducted using a qualitative, interpretive approach. Data for the 2009 study was collected through semi-structured interviews with representatives from the seven political parties that were represented in the parliament before the election (Socialist Left, Labor, Center Party, Liberals, Christian people's party, Conservatives and the Progress Party). Five interviews were made face to face, while two of the parties only had time for e-mail interviews. All of the interview subjects were hired by their respective parties to work with social networking strategies. The Interviews lasted between 40 and 77 minutes, and were taped and transcribed. In addition, content analysis of the SNS' used by the parties were applied. This made it possible to compare what the information workers said with what their employers, the politicians, were actually doing, and to create an overview of the genre system in SNS political communication. Data was collected between March and May in 2009. The genre systems of 2009 and 2013 are presented following the guidelines from [35].

Data for the 2013 election was collected between June and September 2013, mainly through content analysis of the SNS' used by the seven political parties represented in parliament. In total, 6000 posts and comments were collected and a selection of these was coded using the 5W1H method. When no new genres were identified, the remainders of the posts were quickly scanned to see which genre category they matched. Finally, representatives of the political parties was contacted and asked to verify the interviews from 2009. They were given the summary of the transcripts from 2009 and asked if anything had changed in the time between the two elections.

4   Findings

4.1   Summary of Findings, 2009 Election

The interviews made in 2009 identified three objectives for political communication in SNS'. These are dialogue with citizens, contributions from citizens, and involvement in party activities, and are presented in table 1.

Table 1. Political party objectives for SNS participation

	Dialogue	Contribution	Involvement
Why	Involve citizens in debate	Knowledge about citizen concerns	Raise funds. Get people to volunteer
When	Continuous	Election time	Election time
What	Conversation between citizens and politicians	Q&A. Voter stories	Competitions, membership forms, information
Who	Politicians, party members, citizens	Politicians, party members, voters	Voters, sympathizers
Where	SNS, web site	SNS, web site	SNS, web site
How	Encourage dialogue. Open and personal language. Citizen-generated content.	Encourage contributions and questions from voters	Competitions, theme sites, cross-publication

The genres identified in the 2009 SNS' can be analyzed as to which of these "genre objectives" they support (table 2), and this knowledge can be applied by site administrators and politicians in such a way as to facilitate the use of genres which are most likely to lead to the desired objective.

Table 2. Genres identified in 2009 election

Genre	Producer	User	Medium	Related to
Policy comment	Citizen	Citizen, party	Facebook, blog, Twitter, video	Dialogue, contribution
Call for action	Citizen, party	Citizen	Facebook, Twitter, video	Contribution, involvement
Q&A	Citizen	Party	Facebook, Twitter, blog	Dialogue
Appeal to party	Citizen	Party	Facebook, Twitter, blog	Dialogue, contribution
Greeting	Citizen	Party	Facebook, blog	Dialogue
Personal accounts	Citizen	Party	blog	contribution
Video response	Citizen, party	Citizen, party	YouTube	Contribution

Policy comments are comments from citizens on party policy. These come in many forms: Wall or discussion posts on Facebook, in Twitter messages and blog comments. Calls for action mainly originate with the party, but are often distributed through citizens supporting the party making the call. This genre incorporates calls for volunteers, competitions and calls for action in specific cases. Several parties have created Facebook groups for specific parts of their policy. Calls are presented in video, with links to the video posted to Facebook and Twitter. The Q&A genre is perhaps the genre that citizens are least satisfied with. Many questions on Facebook walls remain unanswered, or are answered unsatisfactorily. Some citizens ask why politicians bother having a presence in SNS when they do not engage in conversations with citizens. Appeals to the party are similar to policy comments. The difference is that where policy comments reflect directly on the party's political program, appeals are more specific, asking what the party intends to do with this or that matter. There is some frustration among citizens when these are not answered.

Greeting is an interesting genre. At his birthday, Prime Minister Jens Stoltenberg received hundreds of greetings wishing him a happy birthday. In other cases, we see greetings cheering the party on to fight for a specific case. This genre, while not directly political, could be seen as narrowing the gap between politician and citizen, creating a sense of personal attachment between the two. Personal accounts are mainly found in blogs, as response to politicians asking for the stories of individual citizens. The most interesting example is where the minister of health asks for people's stories as input to a major health reform. Video responses from citizens are rare, but some examples exist. These are typically posted as responses to competitions where parties ask citizens to contribute. There are also responses between parties, where video is used in a similar manner to newspaper debates, and responses between politicians belonging to the same party.

The 2009 election showed an emerging genre system for SNS campaigning. However, there were some challenges identified through content analysis. The main challenge was the mismatch between the expectations of citizens and politicians. Citizens expected answers to their questions and input, but this rarely happened. Responses to party calls for input on specific issues received a lot more comments than other politician-initiated genres, indicating that citizens need to be heard and feel that their input is used for something if they are to participate.

4.2   Genre System 2013 Election

The responses from the political parties did not indicate any major changes in the strategies compared to their responses in 2009. Their ambition to use SNS for communicating with voters stands fast, and is perhaps formulated even stronger. Google+ and Instagram have entered the mix of services being used, but Facebook remains the most important medium for most of the parties, with Twitter coming second. Blogs are not reported to be much used in 2013, while blogging was a popular activity in 2009.

One major change is in the amount of people following the parties and their leaders, as well as a lot more activity in 2013 compared with 2009. Due to space limitations, table 3 summarises the numbers for Facebook only, as this is by far the most used medium.

Table 3. Comparison of Facebook activity 2009 and 2013

Party	2009				2013			
	Voters	Followers	% f/v	Posts	Voters	Followers	% f/v	Posts
Socialist	166 361	1176	0,7 %	111	116 021	13027	11,2 %	565
Labour	949 049	1745	0,18 %	167	874 769	59065	6,7 %	1021
Center	165 006	446	0,27 %	60	155 357	6642	4,2 %	250
Christian	148 748	266	0,17 %	24	158 475	6469	4,08 %	290
Lib.democrats	104 144	1075	1,03 %	100	148 275	12505	8,4 %	546
Conservatives	462 458	1331	0,28 %	194	760 232	26854	3,5 %	928
Progress party	614 717	5835	0,94 %	688	463 560	59980	12,9 %	873

There are some interesting observations to be made from table 3. First, the number of followers and posts made by followers has increased quite dramatically. While most parties in 2009 had less than 1 % of their voters as followers, in 2009 this had risen to between 3,5 % and 12,9 %, which means that Facebook alone reaches a significant part of the voters for most of the parties. Differences in demographics between voter groups could perhaps explain some of the difference between the parties. Activity was also a lot higher in 2013, with a significant increase in the number of posts. Second, there seems to be little if any correlation between the number of votes received and the increase in followers. The progress party is by far the most popular Facebook party, but also the party with the largest drop in votes. While an in-depth analysis of this is beyond the scope of this paper, these numbers nevertheless indicate that SNS could be more valuable for dialogue rather than as a campaign tool. Finally, the numbers from 2013 seem to confirm an increased focus on person over party. The leaders of the three largest parties had had 349 342 (Labour), 89 411 (conservatives) and 119 261 (Progress party) followers, far more than any of their parties. The politicians' activity seems to reflect this, as they share a lot more "private" pictures from their travels. The prime minister before the election, Jens Stoltenberg, published a YouTube video where he posed as a taxi driver, talking politics with the people he was chauffeuring. The video received 1.6 million hits and generated a lot of attention in both social and mainstream media.

Table 4. Genres identified in 2013 election

Genre	Producer	User	Medium	Related to
Policy comment	Citizen	Citizen, party	Facebook, blog, Twitter, video	Dialogue, contribution
Call for action	Citizen, party	Citizen	Facebook, Twitter, video	Contribution, involvement
Q&A	Citizen	Party	Facebook, Twitter, blog	Dialogue
Appeal to party	Citizen	Party	Facebook, Twitter, blog	Dialogue, contribution
Greeting	Citizen	Party	Facebook, blog	Dialogue
Personal accounts	Citizen	Party	blog	contribution
Debate	Citizen, party	Citizen, party	Facebook	Contribution
Support	Citizen	Party	Facebook, Twitter	Dialogue
nonsupport	Citizen	Party	Facebook, Twitter	Dialogue
Link	Citizen, party	Citizen, party	Facebook	Contribution
Disgruntlement	Citizen	Party	Facebook, Twitter	Dialogue

Most of the genres from 2009 are still present in 2013, except for the video response genre, which was not very successful in the previous election. Personal accounts are still present, but not as common. Instead, personal experiences are incorporated into other genres, such as debate and policy comments. In addition, several new genres have emerged. While there was little debate in 2009, 2013 introduces this genre. Citizens provide input and other citizens as well as politicians and the party replies. Support and non-support are other new genres, where citizens show they support ("steady course. Four new years of labour") or not support ("about time someone else takes the wheel") the party. Following the non-support genre is disgruntlement, where those are unhappy with the a party, usually the ruling ones, will present more or less sarcastic comments about the party and attribute a range of unpleasant comments about the party and its politicians. Finally, the link genre simply consists of links to news articles and other sources. This is often accompanied by a short statement ("Do something about this, please!") or question ("Why is this allowed/not allowed"?). Linking to content to support a position shows the richness of digital communication, and the easy by which relevant information can made available to people.

In summary, comparisons of the data from the two elections show that we are moving towards an increasingly rich genre system for political communication. While citizens in 2009 would complain about nonresponsive politicians, this is much less of an issue in 2013. The parties ask for input on a wide range of policy issues, and receive hundreds of replies to issues that people care about the most. This post, from the newly elected government, illustrates the change: "Thank you, everyone who took the time to comment on the government's budget. We have sent all your comments to the PM. Have a lovely weekend". Attached to the post was a picture of the Prime minister holding a sign with a Facebook like button and the text "comments from Facebook". After a few minutes, there were several comments praising the party for listening to its voters.

One challenge which still remains is that the language use within the genres is yet to be consolidated. While traditional channels for citizen and organisational input has relied on a formal language and a set format, citizens providing input through SNS do so with a language ranging from highly informal, with lots of typing errors, exclamation marks and capital letters to the formal language more common in political communication. This can lead to a re-definition of what should be considered "valuable" input by politicians, similar to the argument made by for example Graham [36].

4.3   Towards Politics 2.0?

The genre systems found in the two election campaigns show that we are approaching what can be called "politics 2.0". Several of the seven themes identified by Chadwick and Howard [7] are relevant in this context.

The increase in numbers of both followers and interactions, and the nature of these interactions clearly shows that the Internet and SNS' are becoming a *platform for political discourse*. Political parties have also become a lot better at replying quickly to comments, which further adds to this impression. As for the theme *collective intelligence*, the tone and style of posts made by citizens show that a voice is provided to those who are not usually seen as contributors to public debate. This could indicate that our collective intelligence is extended to those who are not otherwise included in the political process. The theme *perpetual experimentalism in the public domain* shows how SNS' can contribute to more inclusive politics through citizen advice and instant responses. While this theme covers a lot more than the genre and content analysis of this paper, there are indications that this is happening. Parties respond to comments and questions from citizens, and a lot of the posts made by parties are in response to current media events. The theme *small scale form of political engagement* is only present to a limited degree, and was actually more relevant in 2009 with the video response genre. In 2013, there are a few examples related to the use of camera phones, and there have been contests where open government data have been used for creating mash-ups in other contexts not relevant for campaigning. The sixth theme, *propagation of political content over multiple applications*, is very much present, as all of the political parties spread the same types of content across all of their SNS presences. This helps to draw users to content posted on the party's own web site, which makes up a high percentage of the posts made by parties. The final theme, *rich user experiences,* is becoming increasingly visible, and has improved markedly between 2009 and 2013. In 2009, most parties were criticised for posting pamphlets, newsletters and one-way communication, in 2013 all of them present multimedia-rich and interactive content, responding to current issues. When the Socialist party had poor results in the polls, they started their "I vote socialist because..."-case, where politicians and sympathisers made posters citing their reasons for voting and uploaded pictures of themselves to Facebook and Twitter. Info graphics presenting specific policy areas are common, as are pictures and video from various events and links to content posted elsewhere. All in all, these themes contribute towards making politics more personalised, providing access to content and information and could contribute towards a renewal of political interest.

5   Conclusion

Norwegian political parties have used the Internet in election campaigns since 2001, but SNS was first introduced in 2007. The 2009 election was the first time Norwegian parties were expected to really go in for SNS as a campaign tool. A genre system emerged in 2009, and in 2013 the genre system used in SNS' political communication had matured significantly, and the number of users and contributors has increased greatly. The ways in which SNS' are used are moving us towards "politics 2.0", but still further research is needed. Social network analysis could be applied to examine more in-depth how communication flows in SNS', and while genre analysis provides insights into how citizens and politicians communicate, there is still a need to combine this with a more holistic content analysis to fully examine the dynamics of social networks. Finally, on- and offline data should be compared to examine for example if the higher voter turnout of the 2013 election can be attributed to SNS', or if there are other more important deciding factors. Nevertheless, this study clearly shows that political communication in SNS's is contributing to the political parties' election campaign tool box.

References

1. Hestvik, H.: Valgkamp2001.no. Partier, velgere og nye medier. Ny kommunikasjon? In: Aardal, B., Krogstad, A., Narud, H.M. (eds.) I Valgkampens Hete: Strategisk Kommunikasjon Og Politisk Usikkerhet. Universitetsforlaget, Oslo (2001)
2. Name-withheld, A.: study of the 2009 Norwegian parliamentary election (2010)
3. Østerud, Ø., Engelstad, F., Selle, P.: Makten og demokratiet: en sluttbok fra Makt- og demokratiutredningen, p. 344. Gyldendal akademisk, Oslo (2003)
4. Brandtzæg, P.B., Lüders, M.: eCitizen 2.0: The Ordinary Citizen as a Supplier of Public Sector Information. Ministry for Government and Administration Reform, Oslo (2008)
5. Karlsen, R.: A Platform for Individualized Campaigning? Social Media and Parliamentary Candidates in the 2009 Norwegian Election Campaign. Policy & Internet 3(4), 1–25 (2011)
6. Yates, J., Orlikowski, W.: Genre Systems: Structuring Interaction through Communicative Norms. Journal of Business Communication 39(1), 13–35 (2002)
7. Chadwick, A., Howard, P.N.: Introduction: New directions in Internet politics research. In: Chadwick, A., Howard, P.N. (eds.) Routledge Handbook of Internet Politics, Routledge, London (2009)
8. Markoff, J.: A Moving Target: Democracy. European Journal of Sociology / Archives Européennes de Sociologie 52(2), 239–276 (2011)
9. Casteel, P.D.: Habermas & Communicative Actions, pp. 1–6. Great Neck Publishing (2010)
10. Bryson, J.M., et al.: Designing Public Participation Processes. Public Administration Review 73(1), 23–34 (2013)
11. Van Biezen, I., Mair, P., Poguntke, T.: Going, going, . . . gone? The decline of party membership in contemporary Europe. European Journal of Political Research 51(1), 24–56 (2012)

12. Gray, M., Caul, M.: Declining Voter Turnout in Advanced Industrial Democracies, 1950 to 1997. Comparative Political Studies 33(9), 1091–1122 (2000)
13. Rayner, S.: Democracy in the age of assessment: Reflections on the roles of expertise and democracy in public-sector decision making. Science and Public Policy 30(3), 163–170 (2003)
14. Østerud, Ø., Selle, P.: Power and Democracy in Norway: The Transformation of Norwegian Politics. Scandinavian Political Studies 29(1), 25–46 (2006)
15. Effing, R., van Hillegersberg, J., Huibers, T.: Social Media and Political Participation: Are Facebook, Twitter and YouTube Democratizing Our Political Systems? In: Tambouris, E., Macintosh, A., de Bruijn, H. (eds.) ePart 2011. LNCS, vol. 6847, pp. 25–35. Springer, Heidelberg (2011)
16. Boyd, D.M., Ellison, N.B.: Social Network Sites: Definition, History, and Scholarship. Journal of Computer-Mediated Communication 13(1), 210–230 (2008)
17. Anderson, P.: What is Web 2.0? Ideas, technologies and implications for education. In: JISC Technology and Standards Watch (2007)
18. Rose, J., et al.: The role of social networking software in eParticipation. In: Svendsen, S.B. (ed.) DEMO-net: D14.3, DEMO-net: The Democracy Network (2007)
19. Tapscott, D., Williams, A.: Wikinomics: How mass collaboration changes everything, 2nd edn. Portfolio/Penguin Group, New York (2008)
20. Aardal, B., Krogstad, A., Narud, H.M.: I valgkampens hete: strategisk kommunikasjon og politisk usikkerhet, p. 431. Universitetsforl, Oslo (2004)
21. Aardal, B., Holth, I.J.: Norske velgere: en studie av stortingsvalget 2005, p. 381. Damm, Oslo (2007)
22. Chadwick, A.: The Political Information Cycle in a Hybrid News System: The British Prime Minister and the "Bullygate" Affair. The International Journal of Press/Politics 16(1), 3–29 (2011)
23. Hong, S., Nadler, D.: Which candidates do the public discuss online in an election campaign?: The use of social media by 2012 presidential candidates and its impact on candidate salience. Government Information Quarterly 29(4), 455–461 (2012)
24. O'Reilly, T.: What is web 2.0? Design patterns and business models for the next generation of software (2005),
http://oreilly.com/web2/archive/what-is-web-20.html
(cited September 2, 2010)
25. Johannessen, M.R.: Genres of communication in activist eParticipation: a comparison of new and old media. In: Proceedings of the 6th International Conference on Theory and Practice of Electronic Governance, pp. 48–57. ACM, Albany (2012)
26. Shepherd, M., Watters, C.: The evolution of cybergenres. In: Proceedings of the Thirty-First Hawaii International Conference on System Sciences 1998 (1998)
27. Shepherd, M., Watters, C.: The functionality attribute of cybergenres. In: Proceedings of the 32nd Annual Hawaii International Conference on Systems Sciences, HICSS-32 (1999)
28. Päivärinta, T., Sæbø, Ø.: The Genre System Lens on E-Democracy. Scandinavian Journal of Information Systems 20(2) (2008)
29. Sæbø, Ø.: Understanding Twitter Use among Parliament Representatives: A Genre Analysis. In: Tambouris, E., Macintosh, A., de Bruijn, H. (eds.) ePart 2011. LNCS, vol. 6847, pp. 1–12. Springer, Heidelberg (2011)
30. Sæbø, Ø., Päivârinta, T.: Autopoietic cybergenres for e-Democracy? Genre analysis of a web-based discussion board. In: Hawaii International Conference on System Sciences (2005)

31. Johannessen, M.: Genres of Participation in Social Networking Systems: A Study of the 2009 Norwegian Parliamentary Election. In: Tambouris, E., Macintosh, A., Glassey, O. (eds.) ePart 2010. LNCS, vol. 6229, pp. 104–114. Springer, Heidelberg (2010)

32. Yates, J., Orlikowski, W.J.: Genres of Organizational Communication: A Structurational Approach to Studying Communication and Media. The Academy of Management Review 17(2), 299–326 (1992)

33. Orlikowski, W.J., Yates, J.: Genre Repetoire: The Structuring of Communicative Practices in Organizations. Administrative Science Quarterly 39(4), 541–574 (1994)

34. Yoshioka, T., et al.: Genre taxonomy: A knowledge repository of communicative actions. ACM Trans. Inf. Syst. 19(4), 431–456 (2001)

35. Päivärinta, T., Halttunen, V., Tyrväinen, P.: A Genre-Based Method for Information Systems Planning. In: Rossi, M., Siau, K. (eds.) Information Modeling in the New Millenium, pp. 70–93. Idea Group Publishing, Hershey (2001)

36. Graham, T.: Beyond "Political" Communicative Spaces: Talking Politics on the Wife Swap Discussion Forum. Journal of Information Technology & Politics 9(1), 31–45 (2011)

Starting a Conversation: The Place of Managers in Opening Discussions in Communities of Practice

Azi Lev-On and Nili Steinfeld

Ariel University, Ariel, Israel
{azilevon,nilisteinfeld}@gmail.com

Abstract. Online communities of practice are becoming significant discursive arenas in many organizations. Much literature about online communities depicts them as peer-based environments based on user-generated content, where community members take a central role in starting conversations. The current study shifts the focus from community members into managers, and asks who starts conversations in communities of practice, and if there are differences between discussions opened by managers and by community members in terms of scope, topics of discussion, engagement and level of participation. Findings demonstrate the importance of managers in starting conversations and setting the discursive environment of communities of practice.

Keywords: Communities of Practice, Managers, Engagement, Online Discussions, Conversations, Social Media.

1   Theoretical Background

Organizations and systems of governance are characterized by horizontal and vertical dimensions of command and control [16]. Communities, online as well as offline, attract public and scholarly attention due to their focus on the horizontal dimension of governance, which is expressed by peer production, monitoring and sanctioning, collaborative systems of moderation and conflict resolution, and communication between peers [3, 17, 9, 15, 10, 14, 8]. However, communities also have a vertical dimension, which may be even more evident in online than in offline communities. Online communities can have owners, managers, designers, technical professionals and moderators which allow the very existence of the community and perform operations which are essential for creating and maintaining the platform and advance content around which the community evolves and is maintained [2, 14, 8]. But despite the centrality of the vertical dimension in the ongoing activities of online communities, research focuses almost exclusively on their horizontal dimension [5]. This article helps filling the void by studying the vertical dimension of online communities of practice, focusing on the impact of community managers' actions on the dynamics of conversations within the community.

The small literature about management of online communities demonstrates the central role of community managers and their significant impact on attaining the

E. Tambouris et al. (Eds.): ePart 2014, LNCS 8654, pp. 38–51, 2014.

community's goals and on the community's success, in several domains: member management, i.e. recruiting new members, removing members if necessary, encouraging users' engagement in the community [1, 2, 13]; content management, i.e. overseeing the agenda of discussions, initiating and encouraging discussions, facilitating engagement, moderating and preventing "flaming", ensuring that discussions are "on topic" and preventing information overload [8, 11, 12,13]; handling social and technological issues, i.e. clarifying the norms of conduct in the community to members, sanctioning members if needed, and covering other types of administration, such as handling the financial and material infrastructure of the community [14, 8].

Studies also indicate that community members perceive the functioning of managers as critical to the success of the community, and their activity is perceived to contribute to the development from a platform for information sharing to a space where knowledge is constructed through mutual learning between community members [7].

The limited academic literature about the functioning and impact of the management of online communities of practice is mostly based on interviews or studies carried out in small groups. This is, to the best of our knowledge, the first empirical research that focuses on the management of online communities using large-scale quantitative content analysis of more than 7,000 posts. Thus, it contributes to a comprehensive methodological study of the role and impact of managers in online communities of practice- by analyzing their behavior in the community rather than illustrating a perceived importance given to the role of managers, which was the focus of previous research. Furthermore, this study is aimed specifically at learning about the role of community managers in opening discussions, dictating and advancing the discourse in the community. The quantitative data is complemented by interviews with community members and managers, which shed some light on the way members and managers see the importance and role of the manager in the community.

2   Communities of Practice of the Ministry of Social Affairs – Background

The research arena of the current study is the communities of practice established by the Israeli Ministry of Social Affairs. The communities were established in September 2006, to promote learning amongst social workers who are employed in different organizations [4], and utilize the penetration of ICT technologies into the welfare services to promote cross-organizational learning and conversations. Although established by the ministry, most of the members in the communities are not employees of the ministry. In a survey conducted by the website administrators in 2009, only a quarter of the members were employees of the ministry of social affairs, a percentage which is likely even smaller today. The ministry hosts the website but the communities involve practitioners and professionals in positions related to the communities' field of practice from variant backgrounds and positions in municipalities, NGOs and more. At the time of data collection (early 2012), 31 communities existed with more than 7,700 members.

The communities bring together professionals to address issues related to the social services, and function as an arena for encounters between different stakeholders involved in similar endeavors (i.e. adoption, juvenile delinquency, violence in the family and more). Entering the communities requires login using a password, and all communication is identified by members' name and position. The list of members is visible and available to all members of the community, so members know who may read the content they upload, and comment on it. Every community has a manager who volunteered for the mission, and receives a small payback in the form of vouchers [4]. Each day a digest that summarizes the new content which was uploaded to the community is distributed amongst members, to allow them to easily be updated about what goes on in the community, without entering the website itself [6].

3   Hypotheses

Based on the small academic literature surveyed above, the following hypotheses were formulated:

- H1: Since one of the manager's roles is in initiating and advancing discussions, we expect to find that *managers open more discussions compared to members, while members are more active in responding to first posts (relative to the entire content created by managers and members, respectively).*
- H2: Managers are especially vital at the beginning of the community's life cycle, in presenting an example of desired conduct and types of discussions, and in strengthening a sense of community among the members. Therefore, we expect to find that *managers open more discussions in the first year of the community, while members are more dominant in starting discussions in later years.*
- H3: Since all members are familiar with the community manager, but usually not with all of the members, and since the managers are perceived as important and central to the community as previous research suggests, we expect to find that *discussions opened by managers attract more engagement (i.e. more comments) than discussions opened by members.*
- H4: In the same manner, *discussions opened by managers would attract more participants than discussions opened by members*

And finally, at the absence of supporting literature, the following research questions were formulated:

- RQ1: *What are the topics of first messages posted by managers and members?*
- RQ2: *What are the topics of the discussions that follow from first messages posted by managers and members?*

4   Methodology

The study focuses on 11 of the 31 communities of practice which were online at the time of data collection. The communities which were selected for analysis are diverse and present different types of communities, on several grounds: The date of establishment (older communities vs. newer ones), the scope of activity within the community (measured by the percentage of active members out of all members of the community), the size of the community (measured by the number of members in the community) and the areas of practice of the community (therapeutic communities, centered around support to clients, compared to communities engaged in formal issues and procedures). This way, different types of communities are represented in the study, which enables us to learn about the project in general, on its various domains.

After considering the variables described above, the following communities were selected for the study: Intellectual Disability (1777 members), Children at Risk (1549 members), Immigrants and Inter-Cultural Issues (234 members), Blind and the Visually Impaired (554 members), Domestic Violence (1672 members), Foster care (550 members), Juvenile Delinquency (637 members), Community Work (1239 members), Policy and Performance (626 members), Welfare Management at Municipalities (335 members) and Organizational Learning (1558 members). In total, the communities selected for research involve between 234 and 1777 members. Each community has usually only one manager, and in some cases may have two managers.

The research was conducted using a mixed-method approach: A quantitative content analysis of posts from the communities selected allows us to learn about the kind of content posted by managers and by members, and how the communities function with relevance to our research questions. In addition, interviews with members and managers were conducted, which added depth to the results of the content analysis and allowed us to ask members and managers about the way the manager's role is perceived by them, understanding the views behind members' and managers' behavior in the communities.

In each community of practice which was included in the sample, all posts were available from the day the community was established until early 2012 when data was delivered to the researchers. In order to get a comprehensive understanding of the way the communities are used by different types of members, throughout the years of their existence, all 7,248 posts which were included in the sample were analyzed using a coding book which was developed for the study and included 25 sections.

The study involves two units of analysis: posts, and threaded discussions (a first post and at least one additional comment related to it). Thus, some of the categories in the coding book relate to posts and others to discussions. The main focus of the coding book was related to the content of the post or discussion. In particular, the following categories were used to code the content of posts:

- Practical advice, which is directly related to daily work with clients, for example, what is the impact of certain kinds of interventions?
- Organizational advice, related to employees' daily work unrelated to working with clients, for example concerning forms, procedures, programs and courses

- Statements about the community's theme, which are statements that relate not to employees' daily work, but to more general issues related to the community's main theme, for example: How to improve service for patients? How to improve the status of blind people in the Israeli society?
- Emotional support- addressing community members' manifestations of charged emotions (anger, frustration, fear, sadness, etc.) that are related to their work.
- Additional categories were: academic advice, informing on an event or conference, greetings and gratitude, publication of a project or organization, submitting contact details, and finally- other topics.

In addition to the content of posts, other relevant categories in the coding book included time of publication (measured by the time from the community's establishment. For example: Within one year of the community's establishment), and on the discussion level- number of participants in the entire discussion, and number of posts posted to the entire discussion. In addition, every post was coded as being either a regular post or a first post (first posts are posts that start a new discussion and do not comment on a previous post).

The dataset includes 308 first posts by managers of the communities, and 1,201 first posts by the other members of the communities. The study focuses on first posts, because if indeed community managers behave differently than other members of the communities, this would be manifested first and foremost in posts that open new discussions. Although some of the roles of community members as the literature suggests are in intervening in ongoing discussions (ensuring that discussions are "on-topic", for example), we believe that focusing on posts that initiate new discussions can tell us something specific about the way managers dictate the discourse of the community and influence the agenda. The contents of first posts dictate to a great extent the nature of the rest of the discussion. This is where managers and members can have the most influence on the discussion that evolves from their post. Furthermore, comparing first posts by managers and members, and the discussions that evolve from them- in terms of number of responses or participants in the discussion, provides an indication about the relative success of managers to initiate discussions and engage members in comparison to other members.

To complete the picture received from the content analysis, 71 in-depth, semi-structured interviews were conducted with members and managers of the communities, when 5 of the interviewees were community managers and 66 were "regular" members. The main goal of the interviews was to examine how community members and managers perceive the discussion in the community and its effects, as well as their views of the managers and their desired functioning. This can shed light on the dynamics in the community and explain the background of the findings from the content analysis. The interviewees were sampled from the database of the Ministry of Social Affairs, which included exactly 7,777 members at the time of data collection (the beginning of 2012). Community members were selected based on their different scope of involvement in the community, measured by number of times users logged in to the communities, and the overall number of posts they published, in order to receive input from active and passive users, on different levels of involvement.

The interviews focused on usage patterns, views of community manager's actual and desirable functioning, influence of interactions in the community on everyday professional practices etc.

5   Findings- Content Analysis: Comparison of Posts by Managers and by Members

The literature review suggests that a great importance is attributed to the role of community managers, and their functioning can greatly affect the performance of the community and its ability to attain its goals. The general findings suggest that managers are indeed dominant in the communities in terms of content creation. Thus, 17.9% of the posts in the sample were written by managers, although each community, having hundreds to more than a thousand members, has just one or two managers, while only 39.7% of the posts are nested in threaded discussions conducted only among community members without the participation of managers. 51.3% of the posts are embedded in discussions which involved both community managers and "regular" members. In the following sections, detailed quantitative findings illustrate the central role of managers in starting conversations.

5.1   Type of Messages Posted by Managers: First Posts, First-Order Comments or Higher-Order Comments?

The distribution of type of messages that are posted to the communities (first posts, first-order comments or higher-order comments, i.e. replies to comment), may be a result of a few processes that occur in the communities. On the one hand, a relatively high percentage of first messages out of all messages posted by managers can indicate that managers deliberately perceive their role as one of generating, stimulating and "steering" discussions among community members that might have occurred even without managers' involvement. On other cases, a high percentage of first posts by managers may actually indicate a fairly "dormant" community, in which no debates emerge spontaneously and managers need to intervene.

Table 1 shows the distribution of first posts, first-order comments and higher-order comments (comments to comments) posted by managers and members. A chi-square test was performed to examine the relation between the identity of the author of a post (the manager or a member of the community) and the type of posts (a first post, first-order comment or higher-order comment). The relation between these variables was significant ($\chi^2= 38.98$, p<0.01). The effect size was calculated using Cramer's v and was found to be weak (r=0.07). The table shows that managers post first posts and higher-order posts in higher percentages out of all of their posts, compared to the distribution of posts by members, where first-order responses are more common among them.

Table 1. Distribution of posts by managers and members

Author of post	Percentage of first posts	Percentage of first-order comments	Percentage of higher-order comments
Managers	23.8%	26.6%	49.6%
Members	20.2%	35.7%	44.2%

5.2   Timing of Posting First Messages by Managers and Members

A chi-square test was performed to examine the relation between the identity of the author (manager vs. member) of a first message initiating a new discussion, and the publication date of the message- relative to the establishment of the community. The purpose of the test is to analyze whether managers tend to open new conversations more at the beginning of the community's activity than later on.

The relation between these variables was significant (χ^2= 23.67, p<0.01). The effect size was calculated using Cramer's v and was found to be weak (r=0.13). Table 2 summarizes the distribution of first massages by authors and date of publication. We see from the table that managers are more active in opening discussions in the first two years, then in the third year the level of their activity decreases. The fourth year seems to be a more active year- but in the fifth year, again, we see a significant decrease in initiating discussions. As for members, they are most active in opening discussions in the second year, while less active at the first year of the community's establishment. The level of activity in initiating discussions decreases from the third year on.

Table 2. Distribution of first posts by managers and members according to date of publication (after the community's establishment)

Author of first post	Published during the first year	Published during the second year	Published during the third year	Published during the fourth year	Published more than 4 years from the community's establishment
Managers	24.6%	24.7%	14.9%	24.4%	11.4%
members	17.1%	28.2%	19.7%	17.7%	17.3%

5.3   Engagement in Discussions Opened by Managers and Members

In order to learn whether first posts by managers have had more responses in the entire discussion that followed than first posts by other community members, a T-test for independent samples was used. The test found significant differences ($t_{(358.30)}$=3.25, p<0.01) between the amount of comments in discussions opened by managers (mean=5.31 responses, SD=9.78), and the amount of comments in discussions opened by members (mean=3.43, SD=5.5).

5.4   Number of Participants in Discussions Opened by Managers and Members

In order to learn whether discussions initiated by managers result in more participants than discussions initiated by members, a T-test for independent samples was used. The test found no significant differences ($t_{(1507)}$= 0.73, p= n.s). Discussions opened by managers attracted on average 3.42 participants (SD=3.67), while discussions opened by members attracted on average 3.28 participants (SD=2.88).[1]

5.5   Topics of First Messages Posted by Managers and Members

Next, we analyzed the content of first posts (posts that opened discussion) by managers and members. Chi-square tests were performed to examine the relation between the initiator of a discussion and the topics of the first posts. In the following cases, significant correlations were found:

- Practical advice (χ^2= 38.18, p<0.01). The effect size was calculated using Cramer's v and was found to be weak (r=0.16).
- Informing on an event or conference (χ^2= 9.42, p<0.01). The effect size was calculated using Cramer's v and was found to be weak (r=0.08).
- Publication of a project or organization (χ^2= 12.12, p<0.01. The effect size was calculated using Cramer's v and was found to be weak (r=0.09).
- Giving contact details (χ^2= 4.44, p<0.05. The effect size was calculated using Cramer's v and was found to be weak (r=0.05).
- Expressing personal opinions on an issue (χ^2= 26, p<0.01. The effect size was calculated using Cramer's v and was found to be weak (r=0.13).

Table 3 summarizes the distribution of message topics in first messages (messages that opened discussions) posted by managers and members. It seems that messages by members include a higher rate of practical advice, while messages by managers have a higher percentage of personal opinions or publicize events or projects. No significant differences between the groups were found in terms of organizational advice, academic advice or emotional support.

---

[1] It should be noted, however, that the number of participants in discussions where managers were involved (but not necessarily where they opened the discussion) was 4.87 (SD=3.82), and was significantly higher ($t_{(765.86)}$=-4.61, p<0.01) than the number of participants in discussions where managers were not involved (3.93, SD=2.46).

Table 3. Topics of first messages by managers and members (*=significant difference between managers and members)

Topic of post	% in first messages by managers	% in first messages by members
Practical advice*	20.1%	39%
Organizational advice	26.6%	25.9%
Academic advice	9.7%	10.6%
Emotional support	4.5%	3.2%
Informing on an event or conference*	17.5%	11.1%
Greetings and gratitude	3.9%	3.7%
Publication of a project or organization*	23.4%	15.1%
Submitting contact details*	6.2%	10.1%
Expressing personal opinions on an issue*	21.1%	10.3%
Other topics*	10.4%	6.2%

5.6   Topics of Messages Included in Discussions Opened by Managers and Members

Next, we analyzed the content of posts in discussions that followed from first posts by managers (n=1805), compared to the content of posts in discussions that followed from first posts by members (n=4961). Chi-square tests were performed to examine the relation between the identity of the initiator of a discussion (the manager or a member of the community) and the topics discussed in messages posted within the discussion. In the following cases, significant correlations were found:

- Practical advice (χ^2= 65.55, p<0.01). The effect size was calculated using Cramer's v and was found to be weak (r=0.1).
- Organizational advice (χ^2= 4.91, p<0.05). The effect size was calculated using Cramer's v and was found to be weak (r=0.03).
- Academic advice (χ^2= 10.51, p<0.01). The effect size was calculated using Cramer's v and was found to be weak (r=0.04).
- Informing on an event or conference (χ^2= 23.21, p<0.01). The effect size was calculated using Cramer's v and was found to be weak (r=0.06).
- Publication of a project or organization (χ^2= 4.76, p<0.05). The effect size was calculated using Cramer's v and was found to be weak (r=0.03).

- Giving contact details (χ^2= 110.03, p<0.01). The effect size was calculated using Cramer's v and was found to be weak (r=0.13).
- Expressing personal opinions on an issue (χ^2= 14.95, p<0.01). The effect size was calculated using Cramer's v and was found to be weak (r=0.05).

Table 4. Topics of messages in discussions that were initiated by managers and members (*=significant difference between managers and members)

Topic of message	% within messages posted in discussions initiated by the manager	% within messages posted in discussions initiated by members of the community
Practical advice*	32.7%	43.6%
Organizational advice*	27.9%	25.2%
Academic advice*	4.5%	6.6%
Emotional support	3.5%	3.6%
Informing on an event or conference*	9.9%	6.4%
Greeting and gratitude	11%	11.6%
Publication of a project or organization*	8.5%	6.9%
Giving contact details*	1.5%	8.8%
Expressing personal opinions on an issue*	27.4%	22.9%
Other topics*	13.9%	6.9%

Table 4 above summarizes the distribution of message topics in discussions which were initiated by managers and members. Messages in discussions initiated by members include a higher rate of practical and academic advice, while messages by managers have a higher percentage of organizational advice, personal opinions and events or projects publicity. No significant differences between managers and members were found in terms of emotional support.

6   Findings- Interviews: Perceived Importance of Managers and Their Behind-the-Scenes Activity

The analysis so far demonstrates the dominance of community managers in terms of contributing content, initiating discussions and engaging in conversations. In closing this paper, we decided to investigate whether the content analysis findings are compatible with the perceptions of members and managers, and if they perceive a central place in the community for managers, especially with regard to initiating discussions.

The interviews indicate that the members unanimously, recognize that managers are the basis for the community and an anchor for content and conversations. For the interviewees, the managers should develop community discussions even if artificially, maintain the discussion so that it is dynamic and engaging, and act in a way that would encourage members to participate. One of the manager's roles, for members, is to make sure that a shared knowledge relevant to the community's field of practice develops within the community. Some members specified that managers sometimes even work "behind the scenes" and privately encourage members to contribute content and respond (which of course cannot be analyzed using content analysis above).

Z: "if it wasn't for her [the manager]- I, for example, wouldn't even be slightly involved[...] She is doing all she can, trying to reach each and every one of us [...] She is with a hand on the pulse at all times, asking to upload materials to the site."

G: "[the manager] stimulates the responses. I mean that when she writes the first reaction it makes you want to respond more and more ..."

D: "First of all, [the manager] personally encourages the use of the community. [...] She keeps trying to attract people to this medium."

The vitality of the manager for the success and preservation of the community is demonstrated in the words of S: *"I'm afraid if she wasn't there- the community wouldn't exist."*

A sees the importance of the managers in being seen and heard in the community: *"You need visibility. A community manager needs to be seen all the time"*. N agrees: *"You feel like there's someone floating above it all... She puts everything to order"*.

When the manager isn't dominant, members feel the community is dysfunctional: *"Managers of [some] communities are like freelance managers"*, says A., which is a member of several communities. *"They live in a dream world. For me it seems insufficient, their involvement. It's a very technical involvement of a sort"*.

M: *"You needed someone to be more... to be the manager. To operate it for others to be more... it's a fact that it didn't work once the manager was not active"*.

The managers interviewed also reported that they not only post in the community but also act "behind the scenes" to generate content and initiate conversations. One manager describes some of this activity: mapping of relevant and less relevant discussion topics, and attempted to convince members to participate:

"A lot of times I'm asking what [members] read and what interests them, such as what were the things that caught their eyes and they spent more time reading them ... And many times I ask Ok, really I sort of see you less often in discussion groups, is there a special reason for that?"

S adds: *"I emphasize that everything that's being published in the community is important. Input from everyone is important [...] and we take everyone very seriously"*.

The role of the manager as keeping the order in the community was also brought up by managers. A says: *"It sometimes happens that someone crosses the lines. [...] it once got to a point where I removed someone from the community. [...] In some cases, people tried to post comments anonymously. I said: 'In here we all write under our real names. If you're willing to participate with your real name- we'll invite you. If not- then not'".*

7   Discussion and Conclusions

This study is aimed at demonstrating the importance and role of community management and managers in online communities. Despite the widespread perception that social media platforms are driven and controlled by users, which leads researchers to focus mainly on the horizontal dimension of governance in these spheres, the findings of this study suggest that the picture is more complex.

The interviews indicate that community members overwhelmingly recognize the critical role of community managers in initiating discussions and engagement. Even in places where communities were perceived as less successful and fewer discussions occurred, members of the community attributed this to the managers who were less successful in initiating discussions, in members' view. Community managers, for their part, may run into a dilemma: on the one hand they want to encourage conversations and to route them to directions they consider to be vital to the community, and on the other hand, they fear that if they do so on their own, members would not react to the content they uploaded.

However, according to the content analysis it seems that these concerns are unsupported. Content analysis demonstrates the importance of managers in generating content and initiating discussions, and shed light on several important functions of managers:

Managers as Content Producers: Managers are very productive in initiating discussions and uploading content. 17.9% of posts in the sample were posted by managers of the communities, while less than 40% of the posts were part of discussions conducted without the involvement of managers. The percentage of first posts by managers is significantly higher than first posts by members. Managers also tend to open more discussions in the first and formative year of the community, compared to members of the communities.

Managers as Catalysts of Engagement: First messages posted by managers received more responses than first messages post by members. Still, the number of participants in discussions opened by the manager does not differ significantly from the number of participants in discussions opened by members of the community.

Managers as Organizational Mentors: It should also be noted that the discussions that develop from the first posts by managers and members, evolve in different directions. Messages posted in discussions initiated by managers of the communities tended to include more organizational advice and more personal opinions of the discussants. In discussions initiated by the members, messages tended to address topics like practical and academic advice more than within managers-initiated discussions.

Future studies can continue to examine the functioning of managers in comparable online communities of practice. An interesting comparison can be made with less organized communities, open projects not led or organized by a government ministry. These projects may have less structure, and the managers in these communities may be less central and distinguished from other members. It would also be interesting to compare the communities studied here to communities where management is purely voluntary. Based on the accumulated body of knowledge, it should be possible to construct a collection of best practices and recommendations for managers to generate more engagement, trust and sense of community in social media platforms, given the control and influence held by the community managers over the content and dynamics of conversations in these communities.

Acknowledgements. The study was supported by the Center for the Study of New Media, Society and Politics at Ariel University. The authors thank Keren Sereno and Odelia Adler for their assistance in analyzing the data and finalizing the manuscript.

References

1. Bateman, P.J.: Online Community Referrals and Commitment: How Two Aspects of Community Life Impact Member Participation. Doctoral Dissertation, University of Pittsburgh (2008)
2. Butler, B., Sproull, L., Kiesler, S., Kraut, R.: Community effort in online groups: Who does the work and why? In: Weisband, S. (ed.) Leadership at a Distance, pp. 171–194. Lawrence Erlbaum Associates, New York (2007)
3. Connolly, R.: The rise and persistence of the technological community ideal. In: Werry, C., Mowbray, M. (eds.) Online Communities: Commerce, Community Action and the Virtual University, pp. 317–364. Prentice Hall, Upper Saddle River (2001)
4. Cook-Craig, P.G., Sabah, Y.: The role of virtual communities of practice in supporting collaborative learning among social workers. British Journal of Social Work 39(4), 725–739 (2009)
5. Fallah, N.: Distributed form of leadership in communities of practice. International Journal of Emerging Science 1(3), 357–370 (2011)
6. Fein, T.: Online Communities of Practice in the Social Services: A Tool for Sharing and Knowledge Circulation between Employees. MA Thesis, Hebrew University of Jerusalem (2011)
7. Gray, B.: Informal learning in an online community of practice. Journal of Distance Education 19(1), 20–35 (2004)
8. Kim, A.J.: Community Building on the Web: Secret Strategies for Successful Online Communities. Peachpit Press, Berkeley (2000)
9. Kollock, P.: The economies of online cooperation: Gifts and public goods in cyberspace. In: Smith, M.A., Kollock, P. (eds.) Communities in Cyberspace, pp. 220–239. Routledge, New York (1999)
10. Komito, L.: The net as a foraging society: Flexible communities. The Information Society 14, 97–106 (1998)
11. Meier, A.: Inventing new models of social support groups: A feasibility study of an online stress management support group for social workers. Social Work with Groups 20(4), 35–53 (1997)

12. Meier, A.: Offering social support via the internet: A case study of an online support group for social workers. Journal of Technology in Human Services 17(2-3), 237–266 (2000)
13. Osimo, D.: Web 2.0 in government: Why and how. Institute for Prospective Technological Studies (IPTS), JRC. European Commission, EUR 23358 (2008)
14. Preece, J.: Online Communities: Designing Usability and Supporting Sociability. Wiley, New York (2000)
15. Resnick, P.: Beyond bowling together: SocioTechnical capital. In: Carroll, J.M. (ed.) HCI in the New Millennium, pp. 647–672. Addison-Wesley, New York (2002)
16. Sartori, G.: The Theory of Democracy Revisited, vol. 1. Chatham House Publishers, NJ (1987)
17. Wellman, B., Gulia, M.: Virtual communities as communities. In: Smith, M.A., Kollock, P. (eds.) Communities in Cyberspace, pp. 167–194. Routledge, New York (1999)

The Role of a Political Party Website: Lessons Learnt from the User Perspective

Asbjørn Følstad[1], Marius Rohde Johannessen[2], and Marika Lüders[1]

[1] SINTEF, Oslo, Norway
{asbjorn.folstad,marika.lueders}@sintef.no
[2] Buskerud and Vestfold University College, Horten, Norway
marius.johannessen@hbv.no

Abstract. Though substantial research efforts have been spent on understanding the role of political party websites, there is a lack of in-depth knowledge concerning how such webpages are experienced by their users. In this paper, we present an interview study addressing users' experiences of political party websites. Eleven users of a political party website were interviewed to explore their experiences with this website in terms of its features for information, engagement, mobilization, and interaction. The study contributes new understanding of how different features of political party websites affect users' experiences. In particular, our findings shed light on the importance of high-quality informational content in political party websites for user engagement, and the role of features for interaction and dialogue relative to features for information. On the basis of our findings we offer lessons learnt relevant to the design and management of political party websites and suggest future research.

Keywords: eParticipation, political party websites, user study.

1   Introduction

Political party websites have become important arenas for political communication. Through such websites, political parties can present their message directly to the citizens, mobilize supporters during and between campaigning periods, and engage supporters and adversaries in dialogue and debate [1].

Political party websites are typically seen as one component in an online strategy for communication and mobilization, a strategy which may also encompass unofficial party blogs [2], political candidate websites, general purpose social networking sites, and microblogging. Political party websites may connect to arenas for political debate [3] and offer means for interaction with the electorate [4].

A large number of studies have been conducted on political party behavior online [5], including analyses of the features of political party websites, traffic on such websites, and the correspondence between what is offered and how these websites are being used [2,3,4], [6]. Few studies go in depth on how political party websites are experienced by its users [7]; findings of relevance to this topic typically are based on large scale questionnaire studies [8,9]. This lack of in-depth studies on users'

E. Tambouris et al. (Eds.): ePart 2014, LNCS 8654, pp. 52–63, 2014.
© IFIP International Federation for Information Processing 2014

experiences is noteworthy, given that online political communication is hypothesized to improve citizens' political engagement [6] and participation [3]. Arguably, the degree to which online political communication leads to such increased engagement and participation will depend on how the same communication is experienced by its recipients.

In this paper we present a qualitative study set up to explore how a political party website is experienced by its target group. In particular, we studied how the different features of a political party website are experienced. The findings from this exploration strengthen our understanding of the role political party websites may have for the engagement and political participation of their users. Furthermore, the findings imply lessons learnt of relevance for the management and design of political party websites.

The structure of the paper is as follows. First we summarize relevant background from previous studies of political party websites and online political communication. We then present the research question, method, and results. In the method section, we provide a detailed description of the case of our study. In the discussion we review our findings on the basis of the existing literature and suggest lessons learnt for the design of political party websites.

2   Background

2.1   The Evolution of Political Party Websites

The role and appearance of political party websites have changed markedly since their first appearance in the nineties. Norris [3] described how the initial online presence of political parties and candidates, in particular in the United States, generated skepticism concerning its ability to strengthen political engagement. Here, mainstream political candidate websites were seen as mainly supporting uni-directional communication, with little opportunity for dialogue. Nevertheless, in her survey of European party websites of the year 2000, Norris found that about half of these offered an opportunity to join online discussion groups and about the same proportion gave access to volunteer services [3].

The Dean campaign of the US Democratic party presidential primary, 2004, has been seen as a turning point concerning the internet as an arena for political engagement, in particular in terms of mobilization [10]. During the last decade, European parties have introduced a wider range of features and functionality in their websites [6], [11]. Today, the online presence of political parties is seen as highly important to political party's ability to inform, engage and mobilize.

2.2   The Features of a Political Party Website

Lilleker et al. [6] provide a conceptual framework for analyzing political party websites that is useful for our study. This framework was used in a study of party websites during the 2009 European parliamentary elections. The websites were analyzed according to four distinct feature types: (a) information, (b) engagement, (c) mobilization and (d) interactivity. The concepts underlying these feature types correspond to key topics in the literature on online political participation and digital democracy, and are therefore useful as a conceptual framework to study the roles of a political party website.

Information. The information role of political party websites is highlighted by a number of authors [2,3], [11,12]. In particular, political party websites are seen as arenas for direct communication from the party to the citizens, where the party does not have to communicate through the editorial filter of newspapers, radio or television [10]. Such direct communication has been suggested to be of particular value to minor political parties with limited resources [3].

Website Engagement. Increased political engagement may be seen as the ultimate goal of using the web for political communication. In particular in the light of the decline in political interest and organization observed the last few decades [3], [13]. In the conceptual framework of Lilleker et al. [6], the term *engagement* is used in reference to those features of a political party website that are designed to support engagement with the website, such as video, music, pictures, and animations. In particular, such engagement features can be beneficial for the website's persuasive ability. In this paper we refer to this concept as *website engagement*, and discuss users' political engagement as something distinct, or in addition to, engagement driven by website engagement features.

Mobilization. Mobilizing features are understood as functionality that allow webpage visitors to join the party, make donations, or engage in campaigning activities. The value of mobilizing through political candidate or party websites has in particular been made visible in United States presidential and primary campaigns [10]. Functions for mobilization have also increasingly been taken up by European political parties [3], [11], [14].

Interaction and Dialogue. The promise of increased political participation, induced by early thinkers on the political implications of the web, have led to an aim for political party websites to be more than one-way information channels [3], [15]. Norris [3] highlights the potential of political party websites as arenas for dialogue. In the conceptual framework of Lilleker et al. [6], interaction and dialogue (termed *interactivity* by Lilleker et al.) concerns website functionality that support dialogue between the party and the citizens, such as discussion forums open to party officials and citizens alike.

2.3   Approaches to the Study of Political Party Websites

Previous studies on political party websites follow a variety of methodological approaches. A number of studies involve content analysis of political party websites and associated online material [3,4,5], [15]. Others involve network analysis [16] and analyses of website traffic data [2] to map online networks and behavior on online political websites. Yet others use surveys to map citizens' high level usage and preference for political party websites [9] or present interview data from party officials [12], [14]. Some of the studies utilize a combination of different methodological approaches [2].

We are aware of only one previous study, by Baxter and Marcella [7], that go in depth on how political party websites are experienced by their users. This study provided insight in the need for concise and updated information on party policies and candidates, in particular on the local level, as well as insight in users' views on negative campaigning and politicians use of social media.

From questionnaire studies [2], [9] we have some insight in the high level experiences and preferences of the users of political party websites. Nevertheless, such questionnaire studies do not provide in-depth understanding of why these experiences have come into being and how they may be changed, due to absence of in-depth qualitative data.

3   Research Question

Given the assumed potential for political engagement held by political party websites, we are intrigued by the current lack in research concerning how such websites are experienced by its users. We apply the framework provided by Lilleker et al. [6], and propose the following research question:

How is a political party website experienced by its users? In particular, how is the website experienced in terms of its informational content, website engagement features, mobilization features, and features for interaction and dialogue?

The research question was framed so as to target the actual users of the website, rather than citizens in general.

4   Method

To make a focused exploration of how a political party website is experienced by its users, we conducted the study in the context of the website of one of the main political parties in Norway. To gain access to the experiences of the users, we conducted the data collection as a series of interviews.

4.1   Case and Participant Selection

The political party website of our case was particularly relevant to address our research question, as it is set up to accommodate all the four types of website features addressed by Lilleker et al. [10]. The main landing page of the party website resembled any other party website, with features for information, engagement, and mobilization. The party website also included an extensive set of webpages for interaction and dialogue. Some of these webpages concerned local party bodies, others were thematically oriented (concerning themes such as health, employment, education, and integration), yet others concerned political training and additional support for mobilization.

Choosing as our case a Norwegian political party website was beneficial in several respects. Firstly, the high internet penetration in Norway, where 94% of all households have internet access as of 2013 [17], makes political party websites available for practically everyone irrespective of age, education, and income. Secondly, the high penetration of social media in Norway, where 63% of the population visit Facebook daily as of 2013 [18], makes website features for interaction and dialogue particularly relevant. Thirdly, the relatively egalitarian Norwegian society [19] may indicate relatively low thresholds for taking part in interaction and dialogue, which is important for the study of experiences concerning website features for interaction and dialogue.

We invited potential participants to our interview study on the basis of their presence in open groups at the party website. We selected our invitees among people associated with the groups of one or more of five local party bodies. For a person to be invited he or she had to have visited the interaction and dialogue pages of the party website at least once the last 30 days, and not be responsible for any of the party webpages or groups. In total 106 invitations were sent out as personal messages via the party webpage. In the invitations we informed about the purpose of the study, the study administrators, and the privacy policy for the study (such as data management, confidentiality and anonymization, as well as the voluntarity of participation and opportunity to withdraw from the study at any point in time).

We conducted interviews with 11 users of the party website; four female and seven male. Average age was 45 years (SD = 15; min = 25; max = 72). Eight of the participants used the political party website weekly or more. Eight had used the political party website for less than a year.

4.2   The Interview and Analysis Process

The data collection was conducted as semi-structured interviews. The participants were interviewed individually, and the maximum duration of the interviews was 1.5 hours. The interview followed an interview guide targeting the participant's use of the political party website, reasons for visiting, recall of the participant's last visit, positive and negative experiences, causes of engagement, suggested changes, and suggestions for the party's use of the web site in the coming election period. The interview session also included time to browse the website together with the interviewer, which helped the participant provide additional details and also served to uncover possible usability issues in the webpage.

The interviews were taped following the participants informed consent. When all interviews were completed, they were transcribed and analyzed. The analysis was conducted as a content analysis [20], where each interview transcript was analyzed in terms of the four types of political webpage features of Lilleker et al. Following this, the data associated with each feature type were reviewed for common or diverging patterns.

5   Results

5.1   Information

The participants described the political party website as a source of useful and relevant information. They reported to appreciate both static informational content, such as content concerning the political platform of the party, and content of relevance for ongoing events or thematic debates.

M72: For example at the last national meeting there were a lot of presentations you could access. [...] This is a great system. If you have the time, there is no end to the information you can get.

The participants pointed out that the informational content of the party website often is used as part of a broader reading process. For example, when reading about a particular news topic in a newspaper, they might update themselves on the relevant party arguments and standpoints via the party website. Thus, an important role for the informational content on the party webpage may be to supplement news content from other sources and, thereby, provide the party perspective.

M45: Concerning the choice of fighter planes [...] when I started reading about our choice of the Joint Strike Fighter I, I had to, okay, what are the alternatives. [...] And then I had to go back to the party website to refresh my memory on what we used as arguments.

Informational content of relevance to the local party level was seen as particularly desirable by the participants. However, they reported local content often to lack the richness and updated character as they were used to in the content administered centrally, something that was reported as disappointing.

M39: [...] In particular what happens locally. But then, the user experience is somewhat limited concerning what is available of local news. Such as for the webpages of my local party organization there is nothing.

Some of the participants pointed out that the informational content at times is structured and presented in a manner that is difficult to use. This may be due to the informational content being contributed by a large number of authors belonging different local party bodies, and that the information concerns local, national, and international themes. Currently, the central party administration only edits the central parts of the party webpage. A more centralized editorial function throughout the party webpage would have reduced these difficulties, but would at the same time hinder the bottom-up contributions that the website is meant to facilitate.

M25: When no one filters the information, as in an editorial team, it is fully up to the user to judge what the text says. [...] This makes me more critical concerning which texts I prioritize to read.

5.2   Website Engagement

The participants all described themselves as politically engaged, and nearly all reported that their use of the political party website was driven by this engagement. Though some argued that the party website, in turn, could increase their political engagement the main rule seemed to be that regular use of the party website was engagement-driven – not driven by website engagement features. Thus, prototypical website engagement features, such as pictures or videos, were not seen by the participants as critical to build or sustain their political engagement.

M51: I do get engaged by what I am already engaged in, that is, political issues or people that mean something to me, when they are there and tell about something this engages me. [...] But this is because I have a political engagement.

A few of the participants did report that they saw the benefit of website engagement features. In particular, such features were seen as useful in the context of campaigning. Most participants, however, did not highlight such website engagement features as important for their experience of the website. Rather, they claimed informational content presented in an engaging and easy to find manner to be the most important way that the website could support engagement.

Thematic informational content was seen as particularly engaging to the participants, such as content concerning particular issues in health politics, welfare or employment. The participants typically reported their political engagement to be closely tied to a few thematic areas, and that informational content, or debates, on these areas in particular could be experienced as engaging.

F32: [My preference for content] depends on the theme, whether it is a theme I am interested in or not. And if I am interested, a long presentation may be just as interesting as a short one.

Some of the participants argued that for informational content to be engaging it needs to offer a clear perspective, so that it can be seen as a contribution to a larger debate. Neutral informational content is argued to be the domain of the newspapers. Posts and comments formulated in a blend and neutral manner was seen as working against engagement.

The one website engagement feature that was seen as useful by nearly all the participants was email notifications on newly published content. Most of the participants reported such notifications often to be the reason why they visited the party website; without these they would have visited the party website far less frequently.

F36: It is those emails that make me go [to the website] and check. I only very rarely go to check if not.

5.3   Mobilization

The party website was reported to hold a mobilization potential to the participants mainly in two ways: By providing information on upcoming party meetings and by providing information on available training and courses. Information concerning party meetings was seen as particularly useful. Information concerning available training and courses were seen as important to increasing one's own engagement within the party.

F32: It seems like they also take good care of people who want to volunteer to engage more people. This concern for training and schooling is very positive.

Some of the participants argued that the webpages could have been used more efficiently for mobilization at a local party level, and that several local bodies still seemed to rely too much on traditional means of mobilization and not take sufficient advantage of the opportunities offered by the party website.

M45: I was somewhat disappointed when I found out that [my local party body] did not publish meetings online, or enter events in the online calendar or anything. But, of course, I am also obliged to seek such kind of information myself. But it would have been very easy if they just had put it online.

At the end of the interviews, we asked the participants how they would like the party websites to be used during the upcoming campaign period. The participants held that the centrally administered pages of the party webpage could be an important part of a successful campaign, though it was argued that traditional campaigning would be more important than online campaigning also in the near future. Local party webpages were seen as less relevant for campaigning as it was argued that these would require more resources and competency than what was available for most local party bodies.

M38: I think that by no means [the party webpage] can replace work in the field. But it may be an addition to this field work. The problem may be that you mostly reach your own through the party webpage.

5.4   Interaction and Dialogue

Though all the participants had some experience with the features for interaction and dialogue, only two participants regularly used these. These two reported to do so because they were engaged in the topics under debate and wanted to have an impact in the discussion.

Features for dialogue spark off expectations for replies, preferably from party-members in decision-making positions. As lamented by M70, experiences with participating do not always live up to expectations. In this example, he refers to a contested decision with conflicting interests between industry needs and environmental concerns, where he believes the party had taken a stance in conflict with the grassroot-level of the party.

M70: And this issue, I am somewhat upset concerning this. [...] I started a discussion on this to see what kind of response I would get. But, okay, it went as it had to, I am old enough in this game to understand that. But at the same time others reading this might get an eye-opener.

The experiences of the two participants who used the features for dialogue regularly are aligned with the experiences of those who did not use these features much. Three main reasons were offered concerning own or others' lack in active participation through interaction and dialogue.

Firstly, some participants reported to be uncertain of the possible consequences of participating in a debate. Such uncertainty concerned, for example, the degree to which comments should be aligned with the party political platform, or whether opinions in a political discussion online could be in conflict with the participants' other roles in society.

F36: If I was to say anything in an online debate on [this particular issue] I would have to, as I am relatively new in the party, check what I was about to write with others in the party.

Secondly, some argued that debates were typically too bland to be engaging. Posts and comments were perceived not to be sufficiently pointed to be interesting.

M39: You can of course follow [content published by] key politicians, but I find much of their contributions just to be recirculated opinions. I do not even bother to read all of that.

Thirdly, some reported that they saw online debate at more politically neutral arenas, such as the debate sections of online newspapers, as more relevant. Though the features for interaction and dialogue of the studied party website were open to anyone, it was held that politically neutral arenas might include more varied voices and marked differences in opinion and, therefore, be more engaging both for the active debaters and the observing bystanders.

M25: I do not really bother about what the debaters say at the party website. This may sound strange, but they are all inclined to support this particular party. Then you do not get a real debate, like. Then I find it more interesting to read the newspapers.

6   Discussion

6.1   The Role of the Political Party Website

The presented results provide new insight into the role of a political party website by helping us understand how the different features of such a website might affect users' experiences. One noteworthy finding is that the same website may be experienced differently, and thus hold different roles, for different users. This is, in particular, seen for features concerning interaction and dialogue where some participants use the opportunity provided by the party webpage to engage in online debate, others only observe others contributions to the debate, and yet others just disregard the opportunity for debate. This variation in the roles that a political webpage may hold for different users highlights the need for a nuanced framework of website features, such as that of Lilleker et al. [4], to conceptualize this variation.

The role of a political party website for a given user also depends on his or her thematic preferences. Practically all the participants reported that their political engagement was linked to particular topics. From previous studies we know that the informational content of political party websites is important [2,3], [11,12]. This study supplements this knowledge by addressing the need to match the informational content to the specific thematic interests of the users.

We find that though a political party website offers features for website engagement, mobilization, and interaction and dialogue, the user's experience of the website is strongly determined by the degree to which relevant and interesting informational content is easily available. This finding is similar to that made by Baxter and Marcella [7], who highlighted the importance of updated and concise informational content.

Our study participants argue that their use of the political party website is driven by their political engagement, and that this engagement is best fed by the availability of well-crafted informational content. For the bulk of our participants, the main role of the political party website is to provide relevant and interesting information, thereby contributing the party perspective or opinion on relevant themes or issues. This finding complements the perspective of Norris [3] who argued that the democracy-enhancing role of political party websites might be diminished if their only purpose is to contribute uni-directional information.

In our study, it is particularly thought-provoking that the party webpage is experienced to provide limited room for conflicting and diverging opinions. More knowledge is needed on the causes for, and extent of, this perceived limitation in the interaction and dialogue of political parties. One possible cause for this limitation may be individual users' uncertainty and sense of vulnerability when participating in online interaction and dialogue, something that may be strengthened by the relative novelty of such features in political party websites.

6.2   Lessons Learnt

The findings offer useful lessons learnt for the management and design of political party websites, concerning each of the four addressed types of website features. Above all, it is important to notice the need to balance the party website as a space where users can be informed about the politics of the party with the need to provide more space and leeway also for diverging and conflicting opinions.

Information features are critical to a political party website; likely the most important feature type for most users. Informational content needs to be structured in a manner that fits the main thematic interests of its users. Furthermore, to serve its purpose as a complement to other online informational content, such as that of online newspapers, the informational content on political party webpages needs to provide a marked perspective or opinion. Local informational content is important, as this is closely linked to the users' political engagement. Nevertheless, it may be challenging to administer local content so that it is perceived as well-crafted and relevant for the user, possibly due to a lack in dedicated local resources. It will be important to rethink how local informational content is to be produced and maintained.

Website engagement features are second in importance to informational features; at least for regular users of a political party website. This is not to say that website engagement features such as images and videos may not be important to sporadic visitors; in particular, in the context of campaigning. Nevertheless, well-crafted informational content clearly arguing for the perspective of the party is reported to be more important to the user's experience of the website. For sporadic visitors, high level informational content may possibly be an important driver of engagement, as such visitors will need to get a quick overview of the party opinion on political themes of particular relevance for them. Email notifications may be important to bring regular users to new informational content.

Mobilization features are potentially important to regular users of political party websites, in particular for meetings and training opportunities. However, until most party members are regular users of the party website, such features may have to be paralleled by traditional means of information, to make sure that one reaches a sufficient proportion of the intended recipients. Features concerning funding were not at all discussed by our participants. Features concerning mobilization for campaign work were not much discussed either; possibly in consequence of our participants not being part of a party administration in charge of such campaign mobilization.

Interaction and dialogue features are interesting to some, but not all, of the interviewees. It is worthy of notice that such features are seen as relevant also for some of those that do not themselves use these actively. Hence, such features should be set up so as to be relevant also for non-active users. The design of interaction and dialogue features should be done with care, and the purpose of such features needs to be clearly communicated to the users. These features might benefit from having an informal character to signal that contributions can be written and read as spontaneous comments in an engaged dialogue; without differences in opinion there will be no debate.

6.3   Limitations and Future Work

The presented study has generated valuable insight concerning how a political party website is experienced by its users. Yet, given the limited scale and the focus on one party webpage only, the study would benefit from being repeated for a wider range of political parties and contexts – for example within other countries than Norway. We suggest, for future work, the continued use of the framework of Lilleker et al [6] to improve our understanding of what different webpage features means for the webpages' role as platforms to support democracy. Such future studies would also benefit from triangulating interview data with some of the more frequently used data sources for the study of political party websites; in particular, analyses of webpage content and questionnaire studies. The study of users' experiences of political party webpages is important to understand the role of such webpages in a living democracy. We hope our study may motivate future research to continue this endeavor.

Acknowledgement. This work was conducted as part of the research project *NETworked Power* and finalized within the research project *delTA*; both projects supported by the VERDIKT program of the Norwegian Research Council.

References

1. Vergeer, M., Hermans, L., Cunha, C.: Web campaigning in the 2009 European Parliament elections: A cross-national comparative analysis. New Media & Society 15(1), 128–148 (2013)
2. Gibson, R.K., Gillan, K., Greffet, F., Lee, B.J., Ward, S.: Party organizational change and ICTs: The growth of a virtual grassroots? New Media & Society 15(1), 31–51 (2013)
3. Norris, P.: Preaching to the Converted? Pluralism, Participation and Party Websites. Party Politics 9(1), 21–45 (2003)
4. Lilleker, D.G., Malagón, C.: Levels of Interactivity in the 2007 French Presidential Candidates' Websites. European Journal of Communication 25(1), 25–42 (2010)
5. Cardenal, A.S.: Why Mobilize Support Online? The Paradox of Party Behaviour Online. Party Politics 19(1), 83–103 (2013)
6. Lilleker, D.G., Koc-Michalska, K., Schweitzer, E.J., Jacunski, M., Jackson, N., Vedel, T.: Informing, Engaging, Mobilizing or Interacting: Searching for a European Model of Web Campaigning. European Journal of Communication 26(3), 195–213 (2011)
7. Baxter, G., Marcella, R.: Online Parlimentary Election Campaigns in Scotland. eJournal of eDemocracy and Open Government 5(2), 107–127 (2013)
8. Følstad, A., Lüders, M.: Online Political Debate: Motivating Factors and Impact on Political Engagement. In: Wimmer, M.A., Tambouris, E., Macintosh, A. (eds.) ePart 2013. LNCS, vol. 8075, pp. 122–133. Springer, Heidelberg (2013)
9. Lusoli, W., Ward, S.: Digital Rank ‐ and ‐ file: Party Activists' Perceptions and Use of the Internet. The British Journal of Politics & International Relations 6(4), 453–470 (2004)
10. Hindman, M.: The Myth of Digital Democracy. Princeton University Press, Princeton (2008)
11. Lilleker, D.G., Jackson, N.A.: Towards a More Participatory Style of Election Campaigning: The Impact of Web 2.0 on the UK 2010 General Election. Policy & Internet 2(3), 69–98 (2010)
12. Lüders, M., Følstad, A., Waldal, E.: Expectations and Experiences with MyLabourParty: From Right to Know to Right to Participate? Journal of Computer-Mediated Communication, Article First Published Online (2013), doi:10.1111/jcc4.12047
13. Stromer-Galley, J., Wichowski, A.: Political Discussion Online. In: Consalvo, M., Ess, C. (eds.) The Handbook of Internet Studies, pp. 168–187. Wiley-Blackwell, Oxford (2011)
14. Karlsen, R.: Obama's Online Success and European Party Organizations: Adoption and Adaptation of US Online Practices in the Norwegian Labor Party. Journal of Information Technology & Politics 10(2), 158–170 (2013)
15. Jackson, N.A., Lilleker, D.G.: Building an Architecture of Participation? Political Parties and Web 2. 0 in Britain. Journal of Information Technology & Politics 6(3-4), 232–250 (2009)
16. Johannessen, M.R., Følstad, A.: Political Social Media sites as Public Sphere: A Case Study of the Norwegian Labour Party. Communications of the Association for Information Systems 34(56), 1067–1096 (2014)
17. Statistics Norway: ICT Usage in Households, 2nd edn. (2013), http://ssb.no/en/teknologi-og-innovasjon/statistikker/ikthus
18. TNS Gallup: Social Media Tracker (2013), http://www.tns-gallup.no/?did=9107535
19. Østerud, Ø.: Introduction: The peculiarities of Norway. West European Politics 28(4), 705–720 (2005)
20. Ezzy, D.: Qualitative Analysis: Practice and Innovation. Routledge, Oxon (2002); Parliament elections: A cross-national comparative analysis. New Media & Society 15(1), 128–148 (2013)

Conceptualising Trust in E-Participation Contexts

Sabrina Scherer and Maria A. Wimmer

University of Koblenz-Landau, Germany
{scherer,wimmer}@uni-koblenz.de

Abstract. Citizen engagement in political discourse and in democratic decision-making via innovative online means (coined e-participation) has become subject of considerable research over the past decade. However, mass engagement of citizens in online consultation and decision-making contexts remains an unsatisfied expectation. In this paper, we investigate trust as a particular aspect that might influence whether a citizen will participate. Trust is perceived as a complex construct, which is subject of research in distinct research disciplines. To identify and implement measures for increasing trust as well as for minimising distrust in e-participation endeavours, relevant trust relationships have to be analysed to understand implications of using or not using e-participation offers. In this paper, the status of current research of trust in citizen participation supported by electronic means is investigated. The literature review unveils that various implications of trust in the context of e-participation are still not researched well. Existing studies investigate particular aspects of trust. Yet, no conceptualisation of a trust model is available that explains the full scope of trust in e-participation contexts. Hence this paper puts forward such a trust model for e-participation, which builds on the Integrative Model of Trust in Organisational Settings by Mayer, Davis and Schoorman (1995) and the Interdisciplinary Model of Trust Constructs by McKnight and Chervany (2001).

Keywords: e-participation, participation, trust, trust model.

1 Introduction

Several studies have unveiled the importance of trust in e-participation (see e.g. [1–6]). Resulting from the interdisciplinary nature of e-participation [7, p.415], no clear overview of theories and methods applied as well as results achieved so far exist. The complexity of understanding and describing trust in distinct research disciplines [8–12] makes it even more difficult *"to follow and [...] to compare [results in trust research] with each other"* [12, p.28]. To overcome these challenges, the usefulness of a conceptualisation of trust to form a comprehensive understanding is e.g. argued in [12, p.29, 13, p.974ff, 14, p.36].

This work, being motivated by a research grant by the State Rhineland-Palatinate[1], aims at building a theoretical model for scoping trust in e-participation contexts with

---

[1] The research grant "Communication, Media and Politics" (KoMePol) investigates, among other aspects, trust in mediation, perception and processing of politically relevant discourses. The project is divided into distinct sub-projects, where *"mPart - mobile participation of citizens with privacy protection"* focuses on the role of trust in e-participation. More information is available at https://www.uni-koblenz-landau.de/komepol/ (access 2014-05-28).

E. Tambouris et al. (Eds.): ePart 2014, LNCS 8654, pp. 64–77, 2014.

the purpose of investigating the various phenomena of trust from distinct perspectives. The ultimate goal is to derive a trust model for e-participation and to identify the various trust factors in this context. Such a model will help to systematise existing and future studies of trust in e-participation contexts to enable better comparability and better identification of interdependencies of study results and the methods applied thereby from distinct disciplines. This model, together with the systematisation and comparative analysis of existing studies, paves the way for a better understanding of the importance of factors that influence trust in e-participation, which in turn can also inform the design and implementation of e-participation initiatives.

The remainder of the paper is as follows: Section 2 reviews literature to provide the foundations of our research. In section 3, two trust models are exemplified to demonstrate how far they can provide a foundation for a conceptualisation of trust in e-participation. The analysis also shows, which characteristics of e-participation are not represented with these models, and where the trust models need to be extended or adapted for e-participation contexts. As no comprehensive conceptualisation of trust in e-participation could be identified, a trust model for e-participation is proposed in section 4. The model is derived from the findings of exemplifying existing trust models for e-participation. We conclude by arguing the applicability of the proposed model to scope trust in e-participation contexts and by identifying research needs.

2   Literature Review

2.1   Trust Definitions and Existing Trust Models

Due to the complexity of trust as an 'interpersonal and organisational' [8, p.3] as well as multidimensional construct [13, p.976], various attempts of defining [8–13, 15–18] and modelling [11–13, 15, 19] trust exist - both originating from diverse disciplines as e. g. sociology, psychology, political science, economics [15, p.138]. Not only between, but also within the diverse disciplines, no congruent definition of trust exists [12, p.31]. Luhmann criticises that the notion of trust would be often used incorrectly, carrying in his criticism, for example, reference to *"the research on trust or distrust in politics"* [9, p.143]. Following Luhmann, 'issues of trust' might be confused with positive or negative attitudes towards the political leadership or the political institutions, with alienation, with hopes and fears, or with confidence [9, p.143]. The need of one party to trust is defined as a result of some vulnerability to another party; and making oneself vulnerable would mean to take a risk [11, p.712]. Hence, Mayer et al. see trust as *"a willingness to take risk"* [11, p.712] or a solution for specific risk challenges [9, p.144] in difference to other terms as 'cooperation', 'confidence' and 'predictability' by their definition [12, p.712ff]. Another way of explaining the meaning of trust is by using models to conceptualise the scope of trust [12, p.28]. In this regard, two trust models are presented in this section: (1) *Integrative Model of Trust in Organisational Settings* [11] by Mayer, Davis and Schoorman (1995) and (2) the *Interdisciplinary Model of Trust Constructs* [12] by McKnight and Chervany (2001). Mayer et al.'s model has been selected as a prominent trust   model   often   cited   in different areas as e.g. marketing, finance, economics, information systems, political science, communication, ethics, law, psychology, sociology while stemming itself from management and general business [20, p.334]. McKnight's and Chervanny's model is often cited in literature[2], too. Already an earlier version of this model has been applied to study trust in organisations, in e-commerce and in virtual teams [21, p.32]. It has been selected here as it proposes some elements that complement Mayer et al.'s model as we will argue further on, and it has been applied in another e-discipline [14].

Mayer et al.'s trust model focuses on *"trust in an organisational setting"* [11, p.711]. The model presents trust as *"an aspect of relationships"* that *"varies within persons and across relationships"* [20, p.344]. The model involves *"a trusting party (trustor) and a party to be trusted (trustee)"* [11, p.711], and it introduces dynamic trust relationships between both parties. Trust is explicitly differentiated from the activity as a result from risk (i.e. *Risk taking in relationship - RTR*). The decision to take this relationship depends on a function comparing the level of trust to the level of perceived risk in a situation [11, p.726]. The outcome of a risk taking relationship influences factors of perceived trustworthiness (ability, benevolence, integrity) in the next feedback loop – i.e. entering the trust relationship again. Mayer et al.'s model of trust in an organisational setting is visualised in Fig. 1. For details, the reader is referred to [11, 20].

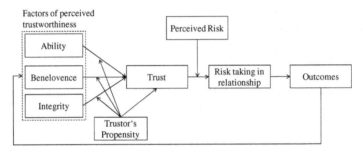

Fig. 1. Mayer et al.'s integrative model of trust in organisational settings [11, p.715]

The complexity of the examined relationships of trust in e-participation makes it necessary to consider the term 'trust' not only from *"interpersonal, intergroup, or interorganisational levels of analysis"* as it is done in the Mayer et al. model [20, p.345]. Trust in *"big ideas, programs, parties, political systems, social changes"* as suggested in [17, p.11] is another aspect to be understood. McKnight & Chervany introduce different perspectives in their 'interdisciplinary model of trust constructs' [12, p.31ff], which are: (a) a *dispositional* perspective regarding trust in general / trust in others, (b) an *institutional* perspective regarding trust in the situation or structures, and (c) an *interpersonal* perspective regarding trust in specific others. Five trust types are classified in these perspectives as visualised in Fig. 2: *Disposition to trust* means the general willingness of trustor to depend on general others [12, p.38].

---

[2] Following Google Scholar, the article has been cited more than 200 times (http://scholar.google.de/scholar?cites=904032774768167641&as_s dt=2005&sciodt=0,5&hl=de, access 2014-05-20)

Institution-based trust means that one believes that favourable conditions exist, which are conducive to situational success in a risky aspect of life [12, p.37]. *Trusting beliefs* describe *"cognitive perceptions about the attributes or characteristics of the trustee"* [12, p.36]. *Trusting intentions* means the willingness of trustor to depend on particular others [12, p.34] i.e. the trustee. *Trust-related behaviour* describes the act that trustor is depending in a situation [12, p.34]. The arrows indicate how these types of trust influence each other. McKnight and Chervany state that these types of trust are supported consistently by empirical data [12, p.40].

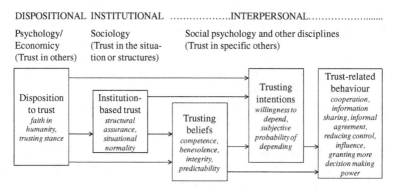

Fig. 2. Interdisciplinary model of trust constructs [12, p.33]

Distrust is differentiated from trust by defining it as separate and opposite from trust [12, p.41ff]. For details the reader is referred to [12, 14, 22].

As McKnight & Chervany's model is influenced by Mayer et al.'s model, similarities are recognisable, for example: (i) Both models refer to trust in general and *"not in a specific situation"*, so the other party is *"the object of trust"* [12, p.34]. Researchers who decompose *"trust constructs into particular trust-related situation segments would obtain indicators of the overall relationship between trustor and trustee"* [12, p.34]. (ii) 'Trust-related behaviour' in McKnight & Chervany's model *"implies acceptance of risk"* and corresponds to the *"risk taking in relationship"* in Mayer et al.'s model [12, p.35]. (iii) McKnight & Chervany express that the *"trustor behaviourally depends on a trustee"*. This gives the trustee *"some measure of power over the trustor"* [12, p.35]. (iv) 'Trusting beliefs' correspond with factors of trustworthiness in Mayer et al.'s model even though Mayer et al. add the factor 'predictability'. (v) 'Disposition to trust' conforms to some extent to 'trustor's propensity' in Mayer et al.'s model. (vi) 'Trusting intentions' can be compared with weighing up trust and perceived risk in Mayer et al.'s model. However, McKnight & Chervany's model extends Mayer et al.'s model by adding more details to comparable elements, by differentiating between 'disposition to trust' and 'trusting intentions' - adding an element to consider institution-based trust - and by not putting the risk as the focal point of the model. The Mayer et al. model looks into dynamics of trust by considering outcomes of a trust-related behaviour and how these influence other trust types. The McKnight & Chervany model lacks such a dynamic view.

To complement these understandings, next subsection reviews definitions and trust models as emerging in e-government research.

2.2   Trust Definitions and Models in e-Government Research

In e-government research, definitions that base on the perception that some party 'is exploited' by another party are criticised e.g. by Bannister and Connolly with the argument that distrust in government would "*not necessarily express a concern about personal risk*" [15, p.139]. Such understanding would rather express a judgement of the government's competence [15, p.139]. Risks could "*range from government imposing additional taxes to State abuse of power, for example by arbitrary arrest and detention*" [15, p.140]. The UN study of trust in e-government uses the following definition: "*trust occurs when parties holding certain favourable perceptions of each other allow this relationship to reach the expected outcomes*" (citing Wheeless and Grotz 1977) in [8, p.251]). However, other scholars see perceived risk as necessary construct in any research model of trust in e-government [23, p.95].

A model differentiating types of trust relevant in e-government is described by Blind [8]. This model differentiates between political, social, technological, moral, and economic trust as well as trust in government. Another synthesis of trust objects, i.e. the objects towards which trust is directed in a situational context is conducted by Papadopoulou et al. [19]. The forms of trust defined there reflect a more detailed differentiation of the model proposed by Blind in regards to technological trust, as trust objects by Papadopoulou et al. are categorised into the following types of trust [19, p.10ff]: trust in stored data, service, information, system, transaction, government organisation, and institution-based trust.

In Korea, a study analysing the implications of Internet usage on trust in government reveals a negative relation of Internet usage in general towards trust in government [3]. The authors argue further that the use of e-government could "*reduce the negative impact of the Internet on trust in government*" [3, p.16]. It is to be tested, whether this also applies to e-participation.

Next subsection provides insights into the status of research on trust in e-participation.

2.3   Trust in e-Participation Research

Current research in trust and (e-)participation consists mainly of studies concentrating on particular aspects, e.g. trust in government or considering the use of electronic tools for political participation. Literature can be separated among researching trust in participation and trust in e-participation.

Trust in Participation. Uslaner & Brown differentiate e.g. the objectives of people for taking part in their communities by types of participation (volunteering, giving to charity, voting, signing petitions, and working for a political party) [6]. The authors conclude that "*trust plays an important role in participation levels, but contrary to more traditional models, the causal relationship runs from trust to participation*" [6, p.868]. They further highlight the importance of the economic context for trust in participation. Grimmelikhuijsen & Meijer investigate if and how far prior knowledge and predisposition to trust government influence the relation between transparency and trust [2, p.151]. No support for a general "positive effect of transparency on perceived trustworthiness" was found [2, p.151]: *"In sum, "naïve" trustees in government organisations lose their trust if government does not do a good job in creating transparency, whereas being naïve has an opposite effect when it comes to perceived benevolence"* [2, p.154]. Another study investigates the hypothesis that public participation enhances public trust. It concludes that *"participation affects [public] trust when it produces high-quality services that the public wants"* and *"enhanced ethical behaviour [integrity, honesty, and moral leadership] on the part of administration"* [24, p.276]. Yet, consensus building alone as a result of participation *"does not lead to public trust"* [24, p.276]. Blind further observed implications of political participation and trust [8] as demonstrated through a relationship diagram in Fig. 3.

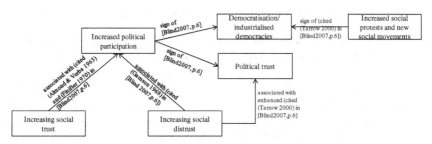

Fig. 3. Relationship diagram visualising dynamics of political participation and trust (derived from [8])

Trust in e-Participation. Kim & Lee examine the relationship between e-participation and trust in local government. Instead of a simple and direct link between e-participation and public trust, the study investigates a structural model for analysing the influence of the e-participation process to citizens' development and empowerment, to government transparency and finally to public trust in government [4, p.826]. Following these causal links, the authors conclude that satisfaction of participants with the quality of government responsiveness and with the usefulness of the e-participation application has a positive influence on the assessment of government transparency and this increases the trust in the local government [4, p.824ff]. Veit et al. prove that trust in an e-participation tool influences positively the expected use and intended usage [25, p.1350]. Coleman & Gotze highlight the importance of moderation and mediation and describe a number of rules for *"trusted facilitation"* of online engagement in policy deliberation [1, p.17f]. Findings by Lee & Kim (2014) would suggest that *"trust in government facilitates citizens to actively engage in citizen-initiated e-participation"* [26, p.8]. Trust in government would encourage their *"cooperation with government"* and stimulate them to take over action.

The conclusion from studies is that the systematisation of the full scope and notion of trust in e-participation appears to be difficult. We therefore return to the trust models presented in section 2.1 and exemplify relevant aspects of these models for e-participation with the purpose to analyse their applicability and restrictions and, therewith, to identify amendments of these models to conceptualise trust in e-participation in a more comprehensive way.

3   Exemplifying e-Participation in Trust Models

The context for exemplifying the models is defined as follows: The trustor is a person interested in taking part in an e-participation initiative. E-petitioning and participatory budgeting were selected for the exemplifications as these are famous and successful e-participation areas, where we gathered a deeper understanding through earlier research. The next two subsections expose the Mayer et al. and McKnight & Chervany models to e-participation. Subsequently, we discuss and reflect the applicability of the models to the e-participation context and derive requirements for a revised model.

3.1   Integrative Model of Trust in Organisational Settings

The main **Risk Taking Relationship** (RTR) in our context of study is that the trustor (the participant) takes part in an e-participation initiative. Various individual relationships may be entered as activity of a participation process e.g. to comment, to take part in a poll, to sign a petition, etc. To analyse **Perceived Risk**, the motivation of the participant for participating needs to be considered (as context information). Here, the motivation is to change a legal/political situation because of personal interests of the participant. Possible direct **Outcomes** of the RTR are that e.g. a petition may have been refused or accepted. Indirect outcomes are for example satisfaction or dissatisfaction with the process, with the democratic system or the influence achieved, with the institutions and groups involved (e.g. government), with the contributions of others, with the ICT from an emotional point of view, etc. For negative outcomes, potential risks need to be identified. For the aforementioned negative outcomes, the following potential risks could be identified for participants (exemplification; further risks may exist):

- Legal/political situation does not change for the participant and therewith everything that the participant has invested (e.g. time) is lost without any benefit.
- User data may be utilised by other parties.
- Participant could experience personal disadvantages as a result of non-anonymous participation through different-minded parties.

If and how far these potential risks are perceived by individual participants depend on the persons themselves and the participation initiative (what impact is possible or expected). The decision to participate might not only base on risks identified. Further a type of calculation between possible positive outcomes (such a concept is not included in the Mayer model) and perceived risks (as condition for participation) might play a role. The relation in the trust model between outcomes and factors of trustworthiness is considering implications on trust as a result of participation. For **Factors of Perceived Trustworthiness**, involved responsible parties influencing the outcomes of the e-participation initiative could be considered as trustees. To all of them, **Trust** relationships may exist if the participant as trustor is aware of their involvement. **Trustor's Propensity** influences trust relationships. Trust in tools or channels is not considered.

3.2   Interdisciplinary Model of Trust Constructs

Disposition to Trust is related to faith in humanity and trusting stance. It is relevant in e-participation to analyse trust in other participants or in the general public. **Institution-based Trust**, which is related to trust in systems and structures, and which differentiates between 'structural assurance' and 'situational normality', can consider trustor's propensity regarding different forms of trust as suggested by Blind [8]: political, social, technological, moral and economic trust (see section 2.1). Trust in Internet can e.g. be explained with the element 'institution-based trust' [14, p.43]. Table 1 exemplifies the roles of different perspectives used in the model for e-participation (based on an exemplification of the model for e-commerce [14, p.42]).

Table 1. Exemplifying the role of trust perspectives

Participant trusts in ...	Trust perspective
decision makers.	Interpersonal, Institutional
platform operator.	Interpersonal
organiser.	Interpersonal
tool used.	
other participants.	Dispositional, Institutional, Interpersonal
democratic structures.	Institutional
Internet.	Institutional
others generally.	Dispositional, Institutional

Trusting beliefs and trusting intentions are related to trustees of type 'specific others'. The element 'trusting intentions' implies some dependence of the trustor towards the trustee and rates the willingness of the trustor for being dependent. In our context, this means that the trustor depends on trustees in regards to the risks listed in section 3.1. However, it would also be possible to express that the trustor is dependent in terms of reaching benefits from these trustees. Some benefits can be expressed as a risk by negation. Yet at the same time, benefits can only be achieved if the participant participates. Some possible benefits can be summarised as: The political situation changes corresponding to participants' interests. The participant took an active role in the decision making process. In Mayer et al.'s model, these benefits cannot be regarded explicitly. **Trust-related Behaviours** focuses on the participation activity and that the trustor depends on the other stakeholders *"with a feeling of relative security, even though negative consequences are possible"* (as it is defined in [12, p.34f]).

3.3   Discussion of the Models' Applicability to e-Participation Contexts

The Mayer et al. model considers influencing factors before a trustor enters a trust relationship. It also shows how outcomes influence again trustor's perception of trustworthiness to the trustee. Factors of trustworthiness can be applied in interpersonal trust relationships and on intergroup or inter-organisational levels [20] so that trust in individual stakeholders and in groups could be examined. The model clearly differentiates trust from influencing factors and from the relationship that is then entered by the trustor. The model shows that, both, the outcomes and the satisfaction with these outcomes influence the assessment of trustworthiness and trustor's further propensity. However, such a feedback to trustor's propensity seems to be missing in this model. Another aspect that is not clearly considered is how a concrete technology or a medium of communication is reflected in the Mayer et al. model.

Assessing the Interdisciplinary Model of Trust Constructs shows some comparable elements with Mayer et al.'s model (propensity to trust, disposition to trust, factors of trustworthiness and trusting beliefs). Beyond that, the McKnight & Chervany model gives insights into trust in general others, trust in the situation and structures as well as trust in specific others, the links between them and their influence in the decision to participate. These perspectives to trust from psychology, sociology and social psychology are to be considered when analysing trust in e-participation. So both models are complementing each other to some extent.

Other aspects of trust in e-participation are not explicitly reflected in the two models: A clear one to one trustor->trustee relationship (on an interpersonal level) is often not existent in e-participation contexts, as there is not only one relationship responsible for the decision of a trustor to participate. Instead, different relationships with different trustees can influence such a decision. Using different instantiations of Mayer et al.'s model or different perspectives with different instantiations of the interpersonal perspective of McKnight and Chervany's model would make it possible to analyse the interplay. As the investigation of these interplays is perceived as important for e-participation, we make an attempt to combine and extend the two models. Considering 'taking some risk' in order to trust and to decide to enter a 'risk taking relationship' is difficult to rate as valuable in e-participation. It remains unclear whether a participant will be aware of risks and whether they would influence participation. Also risk of non-participation might be the same as for participation in the case that the voice is not heard and the political/legal situation is not changed. Here, the key question would rather be, if benefits of participation should be regarded in addition to risks. Introducing considerations of benefits could help thinking positive, i.e. that the trustor would not depend necessarily in a negative way from the trustee. Hence, the Mayer et al. model (as it rather investigates a trust-risk analysis) could benefit from integrating possible benefits. Both models consider in general trust of one trustor in a trustee so that the person is the "*object of trust, rather than the person in one situation*" [12, p.34]. In the e-participation context, the specific situation needs to be considered – i.e. the particular participation experience. Hence the trust object could be 'the trustee in regards to some situational context'. Table 2 shows such trust objects, which have been derived after outcomes have been identified along the exemplification of Mayer et al.'s model. These trust objects limit the dependency of the trustor from the trustee. For example, the trustor does not need to trust the government in general but only in proper processing of the participation input. The synthesis shows that both models can provide an appropriate base to analyse trust in e-participation. However, it is also necessary to add e-participation specific elements as already described above. Next section therefore proposes a trust model for e-participation based on the two models studied.

Table 2. Examples of trust objects in e-participation contexts

Trust in regards to...	Trustee
no manipulation of software (external and internal).	platform operator/provider (PO), general public
no manipulation of hardware (internal).	PO
no software and hardware failures.	PO
data are secured in a safe and encrypted environment.	PO
proper processing of trustor's inputs (e.g. no manipulation, processing in compliance with laws and regularities, conform to descriptions).	organiser, responsible political stakeholders e.g. government
proper moderating.	organiser (moderator)
no personal disadvantages.	government, general public
information provided are correct.	PO, information provider
proper behaviour of other participants.	general public
transparency is provided.	organiser, responsible political stakeholders e.g. government

4   A Trust Model for e-Participation

The proposed trust model for e-participation as presented in Fig. 4 combines the *Integrative Model for Trust in Organisational Settings* and the *Interdisciplinary Model of Trust Constructs*. The Mayer et al. model brings in the dynamic relationships in trust and e-participation, i.e. the relationship between trustor and trustee, trust-related behaviour, which results in outcomes, and the assessment of outcomes influencing factors of perceived trustworthiness. The McKnight and Chervany model adds considerations of trust in others, the situation or structures, and the respective relationships. From the lessons of exemplifying the trust models in e-participation contexts, we add the perceived benefit of a participation action. We rename the RTR in participation as the action since we embark on a positivist approach.

Trustor's Propensity to Trust / Disposition to Trust as characteristics of the trustor describes that „*some parties are more likely to trust than are others*" [11, p.714]. It indicates the "*general willingness to trust others*" [11, p.715] that is further modelled with sub-elements 'faith in humanity' and 'trusting stance' [12, p.38f].

Trustor's Trust in Situation, Structures is based on the concept of 'institution-based trust' [12] with two sub-elements: (i) 'Structural assurance describing that the trustor "*securely believes that protective structures – guarantees, contracts, regulations, promises, legal recourse, processes, or procedures – are in place that are conducive to situational success*" [12, p.37]. In Fig. 4 some forms of trust with relevance for e-participation are listed in this element. McKnight & Chervany exemplify it as "*Using the Internet would have structural assurance to the extent that one believed legal and technological safeguards (e.g. encryption) protect one from privacy loss or credit card fraud*" [12, p.37]. Blind sees trust in the Internet (see also [27]) as one form of technological trust [8].

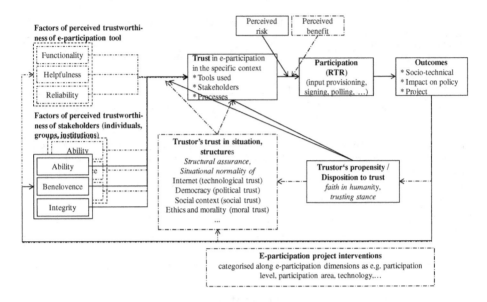

Fig. 4. Trust model for e-participation contexts combining the elements of the *integrative model for trust in organisational settings* [11] (solid lines and boxes) and the *interdisciplinary model of trust* [12] and insights for e-participation (dotted lines and boxes)

Factors of perceived trustworthiness of stakeholders (individuals, groups, institutions) as an attribute of the trustees aims to provide a means for understanding *"why a given party will have a greater or lesser amount of trust for another party"* [11, p.716]. Participation means to take part and to be engaged in a process or act [7, p.402] (individual level). Yet, it may concern also a membership in a group or community [28, p.14] that usually involves a sense of solidarity (institutional/organisa-tional level). The model proposed indirectly deals with this aspect as groups and organisations involved are evaluated for their trustworthiness in this element, which influences trust of participant. Trustworthiness is seen as 'a continuum'. So the trustee cannot be seen as *"either trustworthy or not"* [11, p.721]. Mayer et al. propose ability, benevolence, and integrity as the factors of trustworthiness [11, p.717ff]. The three factors are 'separable' but not unrelated [11, p.720].

Factors of perceived trustworthiness of e-participation tool include electronic and procedural components to the model. In order to consider technology, Plankton and McKnight propose to parallelise *"the three technology-related trust beliefs"* with *"the three most commonly used interpersonal trust beliefs"* [29, p.33]. The authors suggest the following analogies: functionality = ability, reliability = integrity, helpfulness = benevolence [29, p.33].

Trustor's trust in e-participation in the specific context considers all involved stakeholders that might be individual persons (as e.g. politicians) or organisations (as e.g. the particular government). This concept also considers trust in particular tools and processes used in the specific e-participation context. Trust in e-participation is a function of (1) *"the trustee[s]' perceived ability, benevolence, and integrity"*

[11, p.720], (2) *"the trustor's propensity to trust"* [11, p.720], (3) trustor's trust in situation and structures, and (4) tools and processes perceived as functional, helpful and reliable.

Perceived risk *"involves the trustor's belief about likelihoods of gains or losses outside of considerations that involve the relationship with the particular trustee"* [11, p.726]. We add **Perceived benefit** as influencing factor for entering the participation relationship that involves the trustor's belief about advantages and positive outcomes.

Participation describes the action that is taken by the trustor as result of trust. Specifics for e-participation, which need to be included, are e-participation activities. Mayer et al. propose the following function comparing the level of trust to the level of perceived risk in a situation: *"If the level of trust surpasses the threshold of perceived risk, then the trustor will engage in the RTR. If the level of perceived risk is greater than the level of trust, the trustor will not engage in the RTR"* [11, p.726].

Outcomes is conforming to the corresponding concept in Mayer et al.'s model [11, p.728]: Positive outcomes enhance trustor's propensity to trust in others, in the situation and structures, and in specific others. Likewise, perceptions *"will decline when trust leads to unfavourable conclusions"* [11, p.728]. The outcome of trusting behaviour can influence different trust elements; in which form is still subject of research. For the analysis, the evaluation framework by Macintosh and Whyte is proposed, which proposes socio-technical, project and democratic criteria for evaluating outcomes [30, p.21ff].

E-Participation project interventions regard possible e-participation project characteristics that can influence trust. The aim of this element is to provide the possibility to investigate different design decisions in an e-participation project in regards to effects on trust (derived from "Web Vendor Interventions" in [14, p.44]). A starting point for sub-elements can be Macintosh's e-participation key dimensions that are aiming to *"capture any political, legal, cultural, economic, or technological factor that stands out so as to make the e-participation a success"* [31, p.6].

5   Concluding Remarks

This paper has investigated trust in e-participation contexts. The main aim was to conceptualise an understanding of trust in e-participation contexts. The literature review evaluated models for trust in regards to their applicability to e-participation. Two models have been selected for further examination as these are often cited in literature: a) the Integrative Model of O organisational Trust and the b) Interdisciplinary Model of Trust Constructs. To meet the needs of understanding trust in e-participation contexts, the two models have been combined to 1) investigate trust along the whole lifecycle of e-participation projects with a) and to 2) consider different trust perspectives (general, system, individual) with b). Some model elements have been revised and amended to better suit the e-participation context.

Further research is needed to evaluate the proposed trust model for e-participation contexts and the suggested elements and linkages between them through empirical research and through examination against existing theories in other disciplines as e.g. psychology. In a next step, we will define relevant research questions and categorise them using the elements of the trust model conceptualised for e-participation. As the model is currently only reflecting the participant as trustor, further research will investigate the viewpoints of other roles as e.g. trust of administrative agencies e. g. in the input of the general public necessary for starting an e-participation initiative. Overall, this research is also to be complemented with investigations studying distrust in e-participation and whether the distrust aspect will lead to further revisions of the trust model for e-participation contexts. It needs to be investigated how far people's motivation to participate influences trust and the decision to participate, and if relevant elements should be integrated in the model.

Acknowledgement. This work was partially funded by the KoMePol project, a Research Initiative (Stage II) of the State Rhineland-Palatinate, Germany. The authors acknowledge the contributions of and express their gratitude to KoMePol project partners for the discussions of the *Trust model for e-participation*, especially to Rüdiger Grimm.

References

1. Coleman, S., Götze, J.: Bowling Together: Online Public Engagement in Policy Deliberation. Hansard Society (2002)
2. Grimmelikhuijsen, S.G., Meijer, A.J.: Effects of Transparency on the Perceived Trustworthiness of a Government O organisation: Evidence from an Online Experiment. Journal of Public Administration Research and Theory 24, 137–157 (2014)
3. Im, T., Cho, W., Porumbescu, G., Park, J.: Internet, Trust in Government, and Citizen Compliance. Journal of Public Administration Research and Theory (2012)
4. Kim, S., Lee, J.: E-participation, transparency, and trust in local government. Public Administration Review 72, 819–828 (2012)
5. Seligson, M.A.: Trust, efficacy and modes of political participation: a study of Costa Rican peasants. British Journal of Political Science 10, 75–98 (1980)
6. Uslaner, E.M., Brown, M.: Inequality, trust, and civic engagement. American Politics Research 33, 868–894 (2005)
7. Saebo, O., Rose, J., Flak, L.S.: The shape of eParticipation: characterizing an emerging research area. Government Information Quarterly 25, 400–428 (2008)
8. Blind, P.K.: Building Trust in Government in the Twenty-First Century: Review of Literature and Emerging Issues. In: 7th Global Forum on Reinventing Government Building Trust in Government, pp. 26–29 (2006)
9. Luhmann, N.: Vertrautheit, Zuversicht, Vertrauen: Probleme und Alternativen. In: Hartmann, M., Offe, C. (eds.) Vertrauen–Die Grundlage des sozialen Zusammenhalts, pp. 143–160. Campus Verlag, Frankfurt (2001)
10. Luhmann, N.: Vertrauen: Ein Mechanismus der Reduktion sozialer Komplexität. Ferdinand Enke Verlag, Stuttgart (1973)
11. Mayer, R.C., Davis, J.H., Schoorman, F.D.: An Integrative Model of O organisational Trust. The Academy of Management Review 20, 709–734 (1995)
12. McKnight, D.H., Chervany, N.L.: Trust and Distrust Definitions: One Bite at a Time. In: Falcone, R., Singh, M., Tan, Y.-H. (eds.) AA-WS 2000. LNCS (LNAI), vol. 2246, pp. 27–54. Springer, Heidelberg (2001)
13. Lewis, J.D., Weigert, A.: Trust as a Social Reality. Social Forces 63, 967–985 (1985)

14. McKnight, D.H., Chervany, N.L.: What Trust Means in E-Commerce Customer Relationships: An Interdisciplinary Conceptual Typology. International Journal of Electronic Commerce 6, 35–59 (2001)
15. Bannister, F., Connolly, R.: Trust and transformational government: A proposed framework for research. Government Information Quarterly 28, 137–147 (2011)
16. Hartmann, M.: Die Praxis des Vertrauens. Surkamp Verlag, Berlin (1994)
17. Petermann, F.: Psychologie des Vertrauens. Hogrefe-Verlag, Göttingen (1996)
18. Seligman, A.B.: The problem of trust. Princeton University Press, Boulder (1997)
19. Papadopoulou, P., Nikolaidou, M., Martakos, D.: What is trust in e-government? a proposed typology. In: 2010 43rd Hawaii International Conference on System Sciences (HICSS), pp. 1–10. IEEE (2010)
20. Schoorman, F.D., Mayer, R.C., Davis, J.H.: Editor's forum - An integrative model of organisational trust: past, present and future. Academy of Management Review 32, 344–354 (2007)
21. Knight, D.H.M., Chervany, N.L.: Reflections on an initial trust-building model. Handbook of trust research, p. 29. Edward Elgar Publishing (2006)
22. McKnight, D.H., Cummings, L.L., Chervany, N.L.: Initial trust formation in new organisational relationships. Academy of Management Review 23, 473–490 (1998)
23. Akkaya, C., Obermeier, M., Wolf, P., Krcmar, H.: Components of Trust Influencing eGovernment Adoption in Germany. In: Janssen, M., Scholl, H.J., Wimmer, M.A., Tan, Y.-h. (eds.) EGOV 2011. LNCS, vol. 6846, pp. 88–99. Springer, Heidelberg (2011)
24. Wang, X., Wan Wart, M.: When public participation in administration leads to trust: An empirical assessment of managers' perceptions. Public Administration Review 67, 265–278 (2007)
25. Veit, D., Parasie, N., Schoppé, F.: Bürgernahes Regieren: Lässt sich politische Beteiligung durch E-Participation Anwendungen verbessern? In: Schumann, M., Kolbe, L.M., Breitner, M.H., Frerichs, A. (eds.) Multikonferenz Wirtschaftsinformatik 2010, Universitätsverlag Göttingen, pp. 1343–1355 (2010)
26. Lee, J., Kim, S.: Active Citizen E-Participation in Local Governance: Do Individual Social Capital and E-Participation Management Matter? In: Hawaii International Conference on System Sciences (HICSS-47) (2014)
27. Dutton, W.H., Shepherd, A.: Trust in the Internet: The Social Dynamics of an Experience Technology. Oxford Internet Institute University of Oxford (2003)
28. Albrecht, S., Kohlrausch, N., Kubicek, H., Lippa, B., Märker, O., Trénel, M., Vorwerk, V., Westholm, H., Wiedwald, C.: eParticipation - electronic participation of citizens and the business community in eGovernment. Study on Behalf of the Federal Ministry of the Interior (Germany) conducted by IFIB Bremen GmbH and Zebralog GmbH (2008)
29. Lankton, N.K., McKnight, D.H.: What Does it Mean to Trust Facebook? Examining Technology and Interpersonal Trust Beliefs. The DATA BASE for Advances in Information Systems 42, 32–54 (2011)
30. Macintosh, A., Whyte, A.: Towards an evaluation framework for eParticipation. Transforming Government: People, Process and Policy 2, 16–30 (2008)
31. Macintosh, A.: Characterizing e-participation in policy-making. In: Proceedings of the 37th Annual Hawaii International Conference on System Sciences, pp. 10–19. IEEE Computer Society, Los Alamitos (2004)

Information Technology in eParticipation Research: A Word Frequency Analysis

Samuel Bohman*

Stockholm University, Department of Computer and Systems Sciences,
Forum 100, 164 40 Kista, Sweden
samboh@dsv.su.se

Abstract. Recent literature and project reviews suggest information technology is inadequately reflected in eParticipation research. This study uses text search queries to investigate the occurrence of 60 technology categories in a bibliographic database consisting of over a thousand research articles. The results show that eParticipation research have overwhelmingly focused on websites and discussion forums as the main technologies under study. Many other technologies that are frequently mentioned in overview articles as being part of eParticipation have received relatively scant attention in actual research. This article presents findings that may be useful in broadening and deepening the field's treatment of technology.

Keywords: information technology, electronic participation, word frequency analysis.

1 Introduction

Over the last years, a number of literature and project reviews have been conducted aiming to characterize and consolidate the eParticipation field, e.g. [1–8]. The reviews describe a rapidly growing field with research published on a range of topics, including theories, methods, actors, activities, contextual factors, effects, and evaluation. However, technology is inadequately reflected in eParticipation research, being regularly downplayed, poorly conceptualized, or taken for granted. Consequently, there is a need for a systematic review of technology in eParticipation research. This paper aims to address this gap in the literature.

In his analysis of the bibliographical database developed by the European Network of Excellence on Electronic Participation Research, DEMO-net, Medaglia [2] called attention to an inconsistency between the body of eParticipation literature and the rhetoric in the research community. Among other findings, he found that the DEMO-net literature database featured surprisingly little occurrence of the expected eParticipation technologies as suggested by the research community. A vast majority of the database items did not include in title or abstract any of the suggested eParticipation technologies. The self-perception

---

* The author wishes to thank four anonymous reviewers for their constructive comments on this paper.

E. Tambouris et al. (Eds.): ePart 2014, LNCS 8654, pp. 78–89, 2014.
© IFIP International Federation for Information Processing 2014

of the research community was evidently not in line with research results, the study concluded.

This paper is inspired by the previously mentioned study. Using a bibliographic database consisting of over a thousand research items it investigates the number of occurrences of 60 technology categories suggested in the eParticipation literature. For the purposes of this paper, eParticipation is broadly defined as the use of information technology to enhance political participation and citizen engagement. Throughout the text, the phrase information technology is preferred over the lengthier synonym information and communications technology.

To address the research purpose, it is necessary to begin, in a few broad brushstrokes, by offering some clarifications regarding the core concept of this paper, namely technology, in particular, information technology. The accounts and definitions in the following section give an impression. The subsequent section outlines the methods used to conduct the study. The next section presents the results together with some brief highlighting comments. Finally, implications of the findings are discussed together with recommendations for future research.

2   Theoretical Framework

A prominent theme in philosophy of technology is the dual nature thesis [9]. It states that, on one hand, technical artifacts are objects with structural or physical properties that are independent of humans. On the other hand, technical artifacts are objects with certain functions that depend on human intentions and goals. Accordingly, artifacts have a hybrid nature in the sense that they are creations of the mind and of matter. Kroes [9] exemplifies this idea with the engineer's description of a computer mouse. It states that it consists of two X and Y position wheels mounted perpendicular to each other, which functions as a pointing device by sending signals to a computer that controls a display.

In evolutionary, or neo-Schumpeterian, economics scholars focus on the analysis of technological change and the dynamics of innovation. According to Perez [10], the trajectory and diffusion of a technological innovation generally resembles the shape of a logistic curve. At first, changes occur slowly when producers, consumers and other agents of change engage in a collective learning process by exploring alternative designs. Then, when a dominant design has become established in the market, a technology cluster of suppliers, distributors, competitors, institutional arrangements and an accompanying culture begin to emerge, the rate of change accelerates by strong feedback loops in the technology system. Finally, when innovation and growth begin to decline, markets become saturated, and the rate of change decreases and eventually levels out, it provides an opportunity for a new radical innovation and another great surge of development. Perez [10] exemplifies with the current information technology revolution, which began with the Intel microprocessor in the early 1970s. It opened a technology system around microprocessors, their suppliers and early uses in business, entertainment, and the military. This technology system was subsequently followed by other radical innovations, such as the personal computer, software, telecoms, and the Internet, which initiated a flurry of new interrelated system trajectories.

It is interesting to compare the notion of technology in evolutionary economics with how it is theorized in sociology. The core idea in sociology of technology is that technology and society are constitutively entangled. Prominent research programs include the social construction of technology [11], the social shaping of technology [12], and the actor network approach [13]. Briefly put, these approaches emphasize contextual and social dimensions of technology such as the role of individuals, interests, power relations, and economic and political forces. They reject simple cause-and-effect theories of historical, societal, and technological change in which technology is treated as an exogenous force, collectively referred to as technological determinism. Instead, scholars in sociology of technology, for example MacKenzie and Wajcman [12], propose concepts such as path dependency – the idea that short-term contingencies can exercise long-lasting effects – are more rewarding to our understanding of technological and societal change. For example, the history of personal computing provides ample evidence of technological dependencies and lock-in effects.

A more operational definition of technology is suggested by Kline [14], who proposes four usages of the word. The first and most common usage denotes artifacts or non-natural objects manufactured by humans. The second usage denotes sociotechnical systems of production including people, machinery, resources, and processes as well as the legal, economic, political, and physical environment. The third category includes related or partially overlapping concepts such as technique, methodology, knowledge, process, or procedure. The author's fourth usage of the term technology is to denote sociotechnical systems of use, which combines hardware, people, and other elements to accomplish tasks to extend human capacities.

A different view is proposed by Bell [15] who suggests the contemporary notion of technology is routinely used to refer to high technology, things that are new, exotic, and whose "technologicalness" [15, p. 43] is foregrounded or emphasized. Information technology is a typical example. However, after a period of use, most artifacts are normalized, i.e., embedded into everyday life (often through a process of black boxing) and rendered non-technological and mundane.

In the information systems field, March and Smith [16] suggest four broad types of outputs produced by design science research: constructs (concepts), models (higher order constructs and representations), methods (algorithms and guidelines), and instantiations (the realization of an artifact which operationalize constructs, models, and methods). This definition is broad in the sense that it includes constructs, models, and methods apart from instantiations.

Based on a review of articles published in the journal Information Systems Research, Orlikowski and Iacono [17] identified four meta-categories or views of information technology: the computational view, the tool view, the proxy view, and the ensemble view. Based on these four meta-categories the authors suggest five premises for theorizing about information technology artifacts (here presented as four by merging premise four and five):

1. IT artifacts are designed and used by people who are shaped by assumptions, values, and interests.
2. IT artifacts are embedded in specific social and historical contexts.
3. IT artifacts are made up of fragmented components that must be integrated and configured with the context in mind in order to work.
4. IT artifacts emerge from ongoing social practices and evolve over time.

Accordingly, this paper adopts a contextual, multifaceted understanding of information technology. It acknowledges the dual nature of human-made artifacts and that technology and human beings are mutually constitutive. It considers sociotechnical systems of production and use including notions such as innovation, diffusion, learning, technological trajectories, technology systems as well as legal, economic, and political constraints.

3   Methods

A search for relevant scholarly articles was performed using EBSCO Discovery Service that covers over 100 academic databases including Academic Search Premier, Business Source Premier, Communication & Mass Media Complete, Directory of Open Access Journals, JSTOR, ScienceDirect, and Social Sciences Citation Index (Web of Science). The publication date was set between 2000 and 2013. The first search was done on 15 February 2013. The last search was done on 23 December 2013. The search was limited to English language peer-reviewed articles. Title, abstract and keywords/subject terms were searched based on the following key search terms: electronic democracy, e-democracy, eDemocracy, online democracy, digital democracy, teledemocracy, cyber-democracy, electronic participation, e-participation, eParticipation, and online participation. The terms participation and engagement are sometimes used interchangeably, and it appears engagement is commonly understood as a form of active participation [18]. Therefore, both participation and engagement where included using the following additional search terms: civic engagement, civic participation, and political participation, all three in combinations with the terms Internet, web, or online. The searches retrieved 3564 articles. Each retrieved article was manually assessed for relevance by reading the title and where necessary the abstract or full text to eliminate non-relevant items. Articles that addressed eParticipation as defined in the introduction of this paper were saved in Zotero, a reference management software, for further analysis. Duplicate articles and articles that did not include relevant data were discarded. This method retrieved approximately 900 articles.

The search method described above was supplemented by searching the publicly available E-Government Reference Library version 9.4 of predominantly English language peer-reviewed work [19]. The library was scanned for relevant articles using the term electronic participation searching title, abstract, and keywords. The search returned 106 items that were manually assessed for relevance using the same inclusion criteria as described previously. This method retrieved another 50 articles. An additional 30 articles were retrieved by other means, e.g. talking to colleagues, manually scanning reference lists of books and previously retrieved articles, etc. In total, 1004 bibliographic items were selected for further analysis including 728 journal articles and 276 conference papers.

A dozen highly relevant bibliographic items, typically literature and project reviews of eParticipation research, were purposefully selected and manually scanned for lists of eParticipation technologies. This method retrieved 60 technology categories and over 200 associated synonyms and alternative spellings. Based on the synonyms and alternative spellings Boolean expressions were constructed for querying the bibliographic database in order to determine the number of occurrences of the 60 technology categories. Mixed-methods research software NVivo 10 was used for this purpose. In total, 120 text search queries were performed on the literature database of which half were abstract and keywords searches and the other half full text searches.

4   Results

4.1   Literature Review

In the early 2000s, the OECD [20] reported that only a few of its member countries had begun to experiment with online tools to engage citizens actively in policy-making. In a handbook on citizen-government relations, the organization listed a number of technologies in three broad categories: tools for information, tools for consultation, and tools for active engagement or participation in policy-making [21]. Among the suggested tools, we find several that are commonplace today including websites, portals, e-mail, web fora, online chats, surveys, games, and virtual workspaces. We also find a number of tools that would be considered outdated by today's standards such as CD-ROMs and computer diskettes.

The eParticipation research network DEMO-net made several attempts to identify and describe the use of technology for political participation purposes. Macintosh and Coleman [22] suggest a distinction between tools, techniques, and methods for conducting eParticipation and those for studying eParticipation. In the first group, the authors list five main categories:

- Underpinning infrastructures/techniques: open architectures, standards, semantic web (technology, languages, and tools), and agent technologies.
- Platforms/tools: discussion forums, petitions, geographic information systems, web portals, newsletters, question time via email, collaborative environments, consultation platforms, deliberative surveys.
- Design: participatory design, requirements analysis, systems analysis, holistic design, modeling, interviews, soft systems methods, sociotechnical systems analysis, organizational analysis, political systems analysis, multi-criteria decision analysis.
- Content management tools: knowledge management tools, ontological engineering tools and techniques.

- Supporting interaction and comprehension: argument visualization tools, natural language interfaces, discourse analysis, meta- and domain ontologies, dialogical reasoning, content analysis tools, and term extraction.

In the second group, the authors list a number of tools, techniques, and methods for studying eParticipation divided into six main categories. However, most of the tools, techniques, and methods listed here are general purpose social science methods such as case studies, interviews, and discourse analysis. These tools, techniques, and methods, therefore, do not contribute to a better understanding of eParticipation technology and are for that reason not discussed further.

Fraser et al. [23], also part of DEMO-net, list 25 eParticipation tool categories divided in three clusters: core tools, tools extensively used in, but not specific to eParticipation, and basic support tools.

- Core tools: chat rooms, discussion forum/board, decision-making games, virtual communities, online surgeries, e-panels, e-petitioning, e-deliberative polling, e-consultation, e-voting, and suggestion tools for (formal) planning procedures.
- Tools extensively used in, but not specific to eParticipation: web casts, podcasts, wiki, blogs, quick polls, surveys, GIS-tools.
- Basic support tools: search engines, alert services, online newsletters, FAQ, listservs, web portals, and groupware tools.

The authors also list a number of general technologies used in eParticipation tools including hardware, operating systems, protocols, mark-up languages, web browsers and plug-ins, databases, word processors, and streaming media technologies. Further, they mention a handful emerging technologies used in eParticipation including groupware and collaborative technologies, semantic web, agent technologies, data mining, natural language processing, and privacy enhancing technologies.

Tambouris, Liotas, and Tarabanis [24], yet another group of scholars within DEMO-net, suggest an eParticipation tools assessment template consisting of 17 technologies and 17 tools which largely overlap with the categories discussed by [22, 23]. Similar to other authors, their distinction between the terms technology and tool is vague. Indeed, the authors acknowledge, "it is very difficult to distinguish between eParticipation applications, tools, components and technologies" [24, p. 2]. In their survey of EU-funded eParticipation projects, the authors found the three most common tools were content management systems, knowledge management systems, and web portals. In the technology category, the three most common were mobile technologies, XML, and security technologies.

A dozen technologies are identified by Sanford and Rose [1] in their review of the eParticipation field including collaborative writing, content management, data mining, decision support systems, geographic information systems, knowledge technologies, multichannel platforms, ontology and the semantic web, security/encryption algorithms, digital signatures, text-analysis tools, visualization, web logging, chat rooms, and discussion forums. The authors point out that none of them is exclusive to eParticipation, but rather adapted to eParticipation use. They conclude there is no such thing as a dedicated eParticipation technology.

Sæbø, Rose, and Skiftenes Flak [3] see technology as a contextual factor separate from eParticipation activities. The authors note that the Internet is often taken for granted by eParticipation researchers and looked upon as a unitary technology when, in fact, it consists of a diverse collection of infrastructures and technologies. They briefly discuss ten technologies underpinning eParticipation including online forums, geographic information systems, blogs, semantic web, ontologies, data mining, security and encryption algorithms, digital signatures, automated textual analysis, and computer supported visualization. In accordance with other authors, they suggest eParticipation systems are typically applications of established technologies.

In a survey of European eParticipation projects, Panopoulou, Tambouris, and Tarabanis [25] found that one third of the projects used offline channels such as kiosks as a complement to the Internet. According to the survey findings, web portals, discussion forums, and online newsletters/listservs were the three most commonly used tools. Among the technologies, the top three were digital signature and security protocols, web 2.0 features, and mobile/wireless technologies. The authors conclude eParticipation projects mainly use existing, general purpose technologies.

In a comprehensive review of EU-funded eParticipation projects launched during the last ten years, Prieto-Martín, de Marcos, and Martínez [8] point out that while project reports and deliverables typically claim state-of-the-art technologies were employed, the trial systems were, in fact, built on general purpose tools that had been available for several years. The authors found that pilot websites in general were unappealing, error prone, confusing to casual visitors, unacceptable in terms of accessibility and flawed with respect to web 2.0 mindset and tools. Indeed, the authors assert "no real break-through or even any significant research milestone can be reported for the field" [8, p. 247].

4.2   Text Search Query Results

Tables 1 and 2 show, respectively, the top 30 and bottom 30 technology categories in the bibliographic database contrasted with findings of seven previously reviewed authors. The first column lists the technology categories that were retrieved from the literature review. The second to the eighth columns show which authors list which technology. A single bullet (•) indicates the technology was listed in no particular order by the author(s). The numbers 1, 2, 3, and 4 indicate the technology was categorized as a core, an extensively used, a basic, or as an emerging eParticipation technology, respectively, by Fraser et al. [23]. The word top indicates that the technology was listed among the top three in either the tool or technology category by Tambouris, Liotas, and Tarabanis [24]. A percentage value indicates a measure of use in terms of frequency by Panopoulou, Tambouris, and Tarabanis [25]. The ninth and tenth columns show, respectively, the number of occurrences of each technology in abstract and keywords ($N_1 = 964$)

and full text ($N_2 = 1004$) expressed as a percentage of the total number. All percentages are rounded to the nearest whole number. Both tables are sorted by the last column in descending order.

Table 1. Number of occurrences of the top 30 technologies in the bibliographic database contrasted with findings of seven selected authors

Technology	[21]	[22]	[23]	[24]	[1]	[3]	[25]	Abstract & Keywords	Full Text
Website	•							11%	73%
Forum	•	•	1		•	•	48%	7%	71%
Social media								14%	45%
Blog			2	•	•	•	13%	3%	44%
Poll			1				18%	2%	40%
Chat	•		1		•	•	15%	0%	37%
Community			1				23%	2%	31%
Portal	•	•	3	top			58%	1%	29%
Voting			1				15%	4%	28%
Mobile				top			18%	3%	28%
Web 2.0							23%	5%	26%
Game	•		1				5%	1%	24%
Consultation		•	1	•			40%	2%	20%
Mailing list	•		3	•			48%	0%	20%
Petition		•	1				18%	2%	17%
Content analysis				•				3%	15%
Visualization		•		•	•	•		1%	14%
Wiki			2	•			10%	1%	14%
Search engine	•		3	•			38%	0%	13%
Open source				•	•			1%	13%
Survey	•	•	2	•			25%	1%	13%
Newsletter		•	3					0%	13%
Referendum							15%	0%	13%
DSS					•			1%	12%
Knowledge manage.		•		top	•		10%	0%	12%
Identity manage.				•				0%	11%
Ontology	•	•		•	•	•	5%	1%	10%
Groupware	•	•	3	•			18%	0%	7%
RSS				•				0%	7%
Web service				•				0%	7%

According to Table 1, the most common technology in eParticipation research is websites. As can be seen, almost three out of four items in the bibliographic database mention this technology. This is not a surprising result. However, only one author from the early 2000s lists websites as a technology for eParticipation. This result suggests that due to its proliferation, websites have become normalized and rendered non-technological and mundane in eParticipation research. As a result, websites are excluded from subsequent characterizations of eParticipation research.

Table 2. Number of occurrences of the bottom 30 technologies in the bibliographic database contrasted with findings of seven selected authors

Technology	[21]	[22]	[23]	[24]	[1]	[3]	[25]	Abstract & Keywords	Full Text
Instant messaging				•				0%	7%
XML			top					0%	6%
File sharing				•				0%	6%
Encryption					•	•		1%	6%
FAQ		3					40%	0%	6%
Podcast		2		•			3%	0%	6%
Data mining		4		•	•	•	10%	0%	5%
GIS	•	2			•	•	13%	1%	5%
Semantic web	•	4		•	•	•	3%	0%	5%
Kiosk	•	•						0%	5%
MCDA		•						0%	5%
Webcast		2		•			13%	0%	5%
Streaming				•			15%	0%	4%
Text analysis						•		0%	4%
Comp. linguistics	•	4		•			0%	1%	3%
Digital signature					•	•	38%	0%	3%
Social informatics				•				0%	3%
Panel		1					3%	0%	3%
CMS			top	•				0%	2%
Agent technology	•	4		•				0%	2%
CD-ROM	•							0%	2%
Security algorithm				•	•	•	38%	0%	2%
Planning		1					10%	0%	2%
Collaborative writing						•		0%	1%
Open architecture	•							0%	1%
Alert services		3					28%	0%	1%
Online surgery		1						0%	1%
Scenario planning	•							0%	0%
Speech technology				•				0%	0%
Filtering technology				•				0%	0%

Forums closely follows websites as the second most common technology in eParticipation research. About seven out of ten items in the literature database include this technology. Forums are also listed by six out of seven of the reviewed authors of which Fraser et al. [23] classify it as a core tool and Panopoulou, Tambouris, and Tarabanis [25] report its occurrence to nearly fifty percent. Clearly, discussion forums are the most characteristic technology in contemporary eParticipation research.

A notable result is that social media, the third most common technology category in the bibliographic database, is not listed by any of the seven authors. Indeed, the lack of research in social media and its role in political participation and civic engagement has been recognized for some time [7]. However, it occurs in forty five percent of the items in the literature database. It is also the most frequently occurring technology in article abstracts and keywords. Web 2.0, a concept closely related to social media, seems to be similarly partly overlooked in eParticipation research.

Another noteworthy result is that semantic web, geographic information systems (GIS), and data mining are regularly described as part of the eParticipation researcher's toolbox. Six, five, and five authors respectively out of seven list these technologies but they occur in only five percent of the items in the literature database. This discrepancy suggests some fashionable technologies are used for special occasions when it is time to "dress up" and promote eParticipation research.

Table 2 shows the least frequently occurring technologies were filtering technology, speech technology, and scenario planning, along with online surgery, alert service, open architecture, and collaborative writing. These technologies occurred in less than two percent of all items in the bibliographic database. They are also rarely mentioned by the seven authors. A possible explanation why these technologies do not appear more often in the literature database is that they have been inadequately operationalized in this study. It is also quite likely that some of them, such as scenario planning and speech technology, are, in fact, rarely used in eParticipation practice and consequently rarely researched.

Overall, the text search query results show a rather wide gap between what a number of influential studies say about eParticipation technology and what can be found in the research literature.

5   Discussion

Establishing an exhaustive list of eParticipation technologies is a challenging task. This is due to not only the diversity of available technologies, but also a linguistic problem. This paper has shown that the words technology and tool are frequently used interchangeably or in conjunction, typically in the colloquial expression "technologies and tools". Some authors use these words synonymously, whereas others think of them as separate categories. Other vaguely defined and overlapping terms identified in the study are application, channel, component, infrastructure, instrument, method, platform, process, product, system, and technique. A related problem is that many eParticipation technologies are umbrella terms that cover a broad number of technologies that should be studied separately and in their own right. Typical examples are semantic web, decision support system, and groupware. Other technologies, such as social media or web 2.0, have the character of a buzzword. Untangling these phrases and structuring them into a coherent framework constitutes a good candidate for future research as the field lacks common definitions of central concepts.

Based on the results, we can conclude that information technology is poorly conceptualized in eParticipation research. The eParticipation field, it seems, has not drawn much on relevant theories of technology from adjacent fields such as information systems, sociology of technology, or evolutionary economics. Instead, eParticipation technologies are typically conceived informally and simply as tools independently of the political and social context within which they are developed and used. Future research should try to move beyond existing vague notions by analyzing the characteristics of individual eParticipation technologies in detail, looking at both their technical structure and functionality, as well as various levels of contexts and use.

Acknowledgments. This research has received funding from The Swedish Research Council for Environment, Agricultural Sciences and Spatial Planning (FORMAS) under grant agreement no 2011-3313-20412-31.

References

1. Sanford, C., Rose, J.: Characterizing eParticipation. Int. J. Inform. Manage. 27, 406–421 (2007)
2. Medaglia, R.: The Challenged Identity of a Field: The State of the Art of eParticipation Research. Information Polity 12, 169–181 (2007)
3. Sæbø, Ø., Rose, J., Skiftenes Flak, L.: The Shape of eParticipation: Characterizing An Emerging Research Area. Gov. Inf. Q. 25, 400–428 (2008)
4. Chrissafis, T., Rohen, M.: European eParticipation Developments: From Ad Hoc Experiences Towards Mass Scale Engagement. JeDEM 2, 89–98 (2010)
5. Koussouris, S., Charalabidis, Y., Askounis, D.: A Review of the European Union eParticipation Action Pilot Projects. Transforming Government: People, Process and Policy 5, 8–19 (2011)
6. Medaglia, R.: eParticipation Research: Moving Characterization Forward (2006–2011). Gov. Inf. Q. 29, 346–360 (2012)
7. Susha, I., Grönlund, Å.: eParticipation Research: Systematizing the Field. Gov. Inf. Q. 29, 373–382 (2012)
8. Prieto-Martín, P., de Marcos, L., Martínez, J.J.: A Critical Analysis of EU-Funded eParticipation. In: Charalabidis, Y., Koussouris, S. (eds.) Empowering Open and Collaborative Governance, pp. 241–262. Springer, Heidelberg (2012)
9. Kroes, P.: Engineering and the Dual Nature of Technical Artefacts. Camb. J. Econ. 34, 51–62 (2010)
10. Perez, C.: Technological Revolutions and Techno-Economic Paradigms. Camb. J. Econ. 34, 185–202 (2010)
11. Pinch, T.J., Bijker, W.E.: The Social Construction of Facts and Artefacts: Or How the Sociology of Science and the Sociology of Technology might Benefit Each Other. Soc. Stud. Sci. 14, 399–441 (1984)
12. MacKenzie, D.A., Wajcman, J.: The Social Shaping of Technology. Open University Press, Buckingham (1999)
13. Latour, B.: Science in Action: How to Follow Scientists and Engineers Through Society. Harvard University Press, Cambridge (1987)
14. Kline, S.J.: What Is Technology? B. Sci. Technol. Soc. 5, 215–218 (1985)
15. Bell, D.: Science, Technology and Culture. Open University Press, Berkshire (2006)
16. March, S.T., Smith, G.F.: Design and Natural Science Research on Information Technology. Decis. Support Syst. 15, 251–266 (1995)
17. Orlikowski, W.J., Iacono, C.S.: Research Commentary: Desperately Seeking the "IT" in IT Research – A Call to Theorizing the IT Artifact. Inform. Syst. Res. 12, 121–134 (2001)

18. Damodaran, L., Olphert, W.: Informing Digital Futures: Strategies for Citizen Engagement. Springer Netherlands, Dordrecht (2006)
19. EGRL Version 9.4, http://faculty.washington.edu/jscholl/egrl/index.php
20. Organization for Economic Co-operation & Development: Citizens as Partners: Information, Consultation, and Public Participation in Policy-Making. OECD Publications, Paris (2001)
21. Organization for Economic Co-operation & Development: Citizens as Partners: OECD Handbook on Information, Consultation and Public Participation in Policy-Making. OECD Publications, Paris (2001)
22. Macintosh, A., Coleman, S.: DEMO-net: Deliverable 4.2 Multidisciplinary Roadmap and Report on eParticipation Research (2006)
23. Fraser, C., Liotas, N., Lippa, B., Mach, M., Macintosh, A., Marzano, F., Mentzas, G., Rosendahl, A., Sabol, T., Tambouris, E., Tarabanis, K., Thorleifsdottir, A., Westholm, H., Wimmer, M.: DEMO-net: Deliverable 5.1 Report on Current ICTs to Enable Participation (2006)
24. Tambouris, E., Liotas, N., Tarabanis, K.: A Framework for Assessing eParticipation Projects and Tools. In: Proceedings of the Fortieth Annual Hawaii International Conference on System Sciences. IEEE Computer Society, Manoa (2007)
25. Panopoulou, E., Tambouris, E., Tarabanis, K.: eParticipation Initiatives in Europe: Learning from Practitioners. In: Tambouris, E., Macintosh, A., Glassey, O. (eds.) ePart 2010. LNCS, vol. 6229, pp. 54–65. Springer, Heidelberg (2010)

New Ways of Deliberating Online:
An Empirical Comparison of Network and Threaded Interfaces for Online Discussion

Anna De Liddo and Simon Buckingham Shum

Knowledge Media Institute, The Open University, Walton Hall
MK76AA, Milton Keynes, United Kingdom
{anna.deliddo,simon.buckinghum.shum}@open.ac.uk

Abstract. One of the Web's most phenomenal impacts has been its capacity to connect and harness the ideas of many people seeking to tackle a problem. Social media appear to have played specific and significant roles in helping communities form and mobilize, even to the level of political uprisings. Nevertheless the online dialogue spaces we see on the Web today are often re-purposed social networks that offer no insight into the logical structure of the ideas, such as the coherence or evidential basis of an argument. This hampers both quality of citizen participation and effective assessment of the public debate. We report on an exploratory study in which we observed users interaction with a new tool for online deliberation and compared network and threaded visualizations of arguments. Results of the study suggest that network visualization of arguments can effectively improve online debate by facilitating higher-level inferences and making the debate more engaging and fun.

Keywords: Argumentation, Computer Supported Argument Visualisation (CSAV), Online Deliberation, Collective Intelligence.

1   Introduction

Online debate through social media is increasingly used to promote citizens' engagement in policy and decision-making. While common social media websites reach increasing number of users all around the globe, and successfully respond to the demand of scaling up citizen access to public debate [1], the way in which those tools support discourse structuring, representation and analysis remains quite limited [2, 3]. This hampers the very quality of citizen participation to the public discourse and undermines the impact of citizen contributions to e-government and e-participation processes. We argue that one of the main barriers to quality e-participation to public debate is the lack of support for discourse reading and understanding. It is hardly possible for citizens to quickly grasp the main issues involved in an online debate, understand the articulation of the arguments presented, and discovering emerging synergies and conflicts.

E. Tambouris et al. (Eds.): ePart 2014, LNCS 8654, pp. 90–101, 2014.

In this paper we present results of an exploratory study, which suggests that network visualization of arguments can effectively improve the way in which users read and understand online discourse in at least two ways:

- by facilitating higher-level inferences of how the online discourse contents relate; and
- by supporting the identification of argumentation chains, synergies and contrasts within the discourse.

Moreover, we observed that the dynamic animation of networks adds an element of fun and excitement to arguments exploration. This may play an important role in promoting users' engagements with the online debate, especially crucial for motivating younger citizens.

In the following we detail the results of the study, starting from describing background knowledge and motivating the research in the CSAV (Computer Supported Argument Visualization) and Online Deliberation literature (section 2). We describe the research question and method (section 3), report on the user study (design, and experimentation setting), and describe the tool used to investigate the research question (section 4). Finally we discuss the data analysis and interpretation and present main research findings (Section 5). We conclude by outlining potential applications and future research (section 6).

2   Background and Motivation

2.1   Background Knowledge: Computer Supported Argument Visualization for Online Deliberation

The rationale and motivation for this work have roots at the intersection of Computer Supported Argument Visualization (CSAV) and Online Deliberation (OD) research, which studies how computer mediated communication can be combined with argumentation theory to enhance public deliberation. We aim to investigate how multidimensional communication flows (between people, environments, time, topics and points of views) can be translated into coherent discourse and eventually lead groups to better understanding "wicked problems" [4]. Wicked problems are undetermined and complex by nature, and they require deliberative discussions and argumentation to be better understood and tackled. Supporting better understanding and deliberating is the first steps toward the development of informed participation to policy and decision-making, and it therefore sits at the art of e-participation research.

Computer Supported Cooperative Work (CSCW) and Computer supported Collaborative Argumentation have been recognized as two major areas of research that provide support for e-consultation (pp 53, [5]). Many projects prove the extent of interest and research in this area and its relevance to develop new technologies for e-participation (for a review of argumentation tools for e-participations see [6, 7]). CSAV tools have proved to encourage debate and deliberation by citizens on public issues and have been applied f.i for policy formulation to provide a visual medium by which citizens can follow and join in public debates on policy issues [8].

Tambouris et al. even identify CSAV between the key enabling characteristics to consider when assessing eParticipation projects and tools [9].

Computer Supported Argument Visualization (CSAV) aims to augment the personal and collective ability of users to explore complex problems, make sense of difference in viewpoints, discuss options, and reflect on the implication of those by analyzing and constructing arguments.

CSAV is a research field which has its roots that span several disciplines, such as Philosophy, HCI, hypertext, CMC, and several domain applications, such as design, education, law and public policy [10]. The idea that people can augment their human intellect and their capability to "comprehend and find solution to complex-problem solving situations" by manipulating explicit and externalized "concept structures" dates to Douglas Engelbart [11]. Concept Mapping [12] and Argument Mapping [13] have been applied to support education and critical thinking and several authors identified "visualization" as an important but unexploited dimension for refining and communicating one's thoughts [14]. Argumentation and the associated technological support for argument analysis and construction, have been widely investigated in the two decades from the 70ies and 90ies, when first class researchers in the hypertext community developed prototype tools (between others NoteCards [15], gIBIS [13] and AAA [16]) and carried out pilot studies to explore advantages and shortcoming of this approach [17]

In design rationale studies several limitations have been identified which highlights the difficulty to use computer supported argumentation for design practice, particularly related to the conceptual and time overheads in fragmenting and structuring thoughts before communication. Fisher and al. [18] suggest that there are many limitations that need to be overcome to make argumentation (and argumentation tools) serve design; and these concerns have been echoed in [19].

Nonetheless, in another domains such as Technology Enhanced Learning, Public engagement and e-Participation the interest in argumentation and CSAV has persistently been followed, also encouraged by the recognized advantages of this approach in term of support to reflection, knowledge construction and learning [20]. Example tools for large-scale deliberation are currently classified as e-participation, e-democracy or e-government systems [21, 22] some of which uses CSAV as a way to structure and facilitate citizens consultation [8] and large scale participation to public debates [23].

An established research literature documents the advantages of making the structure and status of a dialogue or debate more visible [10]. Scheuer and al. [24] review the state of the art of computer-supported argumentation, which proves the extensive interest and production of research and technology in this field. Scheuer and al. present a rich overview of both the types of argument representations, as well as the variety of interaction designs and ontologies to support argumentation. Several empirical studies are also presented that have been carried out to assess various argumentation systems in different domains. While many of these systems are aimed to support argumentation in a learning context [25](e.g Belvedere [26] and ARGUNAUTUT [27]); many others have been designed to support argumentation in other fields such as law (Carneades [28] and Rationale [29]; science (SenseMaker [30], WISE [31]) and decision making (QuestMap, Compendium [32, 33]).

We are interested in this last category of argumentation systems and their Web successors which have been designed to support e-democracy and e-participation by promoting citizen engagements in decision-making throughout online discourse processes. These are specifically designed collective intelligence infrastructures and large-scale argumentation systems to structure informal online discussion as argumentation processes and use CSAV to makes visually explicit users' lines of reasoning and (dis)agreements [34]. Naturally, the use of semantic networks to provide computational intelligence has now converged with Web Science, resulting in Web 2.0 Argumentation [35] and a semantic web standards-based Argument Web [36].

2.2   Research Gap and Motivation

Many of these CSAV tools are now available, exhibiting a wide mix of network visualizations and more conventional threaded renderings. Whereas many systems use a common ontology to represent discourse element (such as IBIS [4] or its more design oriented version QOC [37], when it gets to argument visualization there seems to be no agreement on what is the best interface for argument visualization. Deliberatorium uses a linear-threaded visualization [3], while Cohere [35] supports a graph visualization of the online discourse. Debategraph[1] and CoPe_it! [38] enable linear, threaded and graph views. However, to date, we have not yet found a systematic evaluation of the merits or otherwise of CSAV vs. threaded interfaces.

In addition to this, the suitability of graphs as medium to support argumentation has been questioned by some, for three main reasons: complexity of the ontology, number of participants and domain of application. Some researchers argue that the bigger the number of participants to the discussion, and the higher the complexity of the discourse ontology, more clumsy and less usable graph visualizations become (pp.53 [24]). In addition, there seems to be resistance to the use of graph visualization of arguments in certain domains of application. Hair [39] reports on a study in the legal field in which lawyers have expressed a strong preference in favour of linear-threaded text representations of arguments compared to network visualization.

It therefore remains unclear what are the advantages and affordances of different graphical representation of arguments to support online discussion and large-scale deliberation. This motivates the research presented in this paper.

An exploratory user study was carried out to compare network visualizations and threaded discussions as the two most commonly used interfaces for argument visualization. We aimed to assess which one of these two visualizations better support online discourse in two main tasks: argumentation reading and understanding. Argumentation reading and understanding are at the cornerstone of effective participation to online discourse, and they also consist of the most prominent users interaction modality. In fact, the internet usage pattern of "participation inequality"

---

[1] DebateGraph 2013: Web tool for the visualization of idea and debates
http://debategraph.org

[40] confirms that typically, only a very small percentage of users contributes to a website, compared to vast majority who consume. So, while browsing, searching, reading and writing clearly cannot be divorced from each other, the focus of the study reported here is not on the authoring process, but on the experience and performance of the majority of users who will be reading and searching the online deliberation platforms.

3   Research Question and Methodology

Does an interactive, self-organizing network visualization of arguments provide advantages over a more conventional threaded interface for reading and search? The following research questions was formulated:

RQ: What are the recognized advantages of threaded and network visualization of arguments for supporting online discourse reading and understanding?

A grounded theory analysis has been conducted to study the use of different graphical interfaces for the representation of arguments, and to assess to what extend these affect the way in which users read and understand the online discourse. Grounded Theory is a qualitative research method which has been widely used in HCI to provide insights on people's views, behaviors, understanding and experience with technology [41]. Very recently the discussion has been revamped on what are the nuances and innovation to the method that may help to respond to the increasing request and diffusion of qualitative research studies in HCI [42].

We took a 'constructivist' stance to grounded theory which aims at creating a description of the context rather than discovering a description of it (objectivist approach). We started by keeping a Glaserian approach to data analysis and applied open coding of the data trying not to be influenced by prior ideas or extant theories. The initial open coding phase was performed on transcripts of the screencast video of users' interaction in the experimentation. Video clips and transcripts were analyzed and coded in an unfocused manner. While reiterating the coding from one user experimentation to the following, we moved progressively to a more focused coding in which specific concepts and themes started emerging. From this analysis several categories emerged which provided the building blocks of our findings, and the main pillars of our narrative of the analyzed phenomenon.

The coding process generated over 350 codes, which have been edited and merged in several revising cycles, and then have been grouped into main sub-categories (23 in total) and higher-level categories of analysis (9 in total). The main higher-level categories emerged provided a taxonomy of the main components/variables which effect users capabilities to read and comprehend online argumentative discussion. The 9 categories have then been ordered on the base of what were more significant in terms of three metrics: number of quotations per code (N. of Videoclips/Quotation), number of participants who experienced the event captures by the code (N. of People affected), and time of interaction per code. As a result three main higher-level code categories emerged as key factors affecting users interaction and these have been used as metrics to access users performance with the two interfaces (see section 5).

We then developed a narrative around these 3 emerging themes, but also around events and findings, rooted in the in depth observation and analysis of the interaction. This allowed us to draw some conclusions on what are the recognized advantages of threaded and network visualization of arguments to support online discourse reading and understanding.

4   User Study

4.1   Goal, Design and Participants

We studied an heterogeneous group of researchers and practitioners in Higher Education engaged in the use of a collective intelligence tool for collaborative argumentative discourse and knowledge construction. An exploratory user study was run to observe users' performance under three information-seeking tasks, and compare their performances using two different user interfaces for arguments visualization (threaded vs network visualization of arguments). Participants were divided in two groups of 5 (Group1 and Group2). The 10 subjects were drawn from the members of different Open University departments, so with widely mixed IT expertise. They were randomly allocated to the two different groups, but we verified post-hoc that IT expert/non ex-pert ratio in each group was approximately the same. The median age was 40 (with range from 32 to 48) with the majority of users being either native or near-native English speakers.

4.2   Online Environment: The Evidence Hub

The online discussion tool used throughout the study was the Evidence Hub system[43]. The Evidence Hub is a collective intelligence and online deliberation tool to support argumentative knowledge construction by crowdsourcing contributions of issues, potential solutions, research claims and the related evidence in favor or against those. The Evidence Hub is particularly oriented to support community of practitioners to build evidence-based knowledge about specific key challenges that are set up to the community. This key challenges can then be addressed by tackling specific sub issues, that the community contribute to add to the system. Each sub issue can then be tackled by proposing solutions to it, or by sharing specific research claims that can help tackling the issue. Finally potential solutions and research claims can be debated by the community by advancing evidence in favor or against those and by providing relative resources backing them up. By scaffolding users contributions in this way, the Evidence Hub aim to effectively crowdsource and support large-scale deliberation in e-democracy and decision-making processes. To allow comparison between users interaction with two graphical representations of arguments, two different versions of the Evidence Hub have been set up which used different user interfaces for arguments visualization. The two versions of the Evidence Hub pointed at the same database to ensure that participants in the two groups would receive the same quantity and type of information.

4.3   The Linear-Threaded Interface for Arguments Visualization

The linear-threaded interface was used by Group1 (Figure 1). This interface for arguments visualization is similar to the most common threaded online discussion interfaces to support argumentative discourse activities. It consists of a classical threaded visualization in which issues set the focus of discussion (title of the page in Figure 1), and then potential solutions are listed below (light bulb icons are placed before each solution). Each solution can then be expanded on demand. The progressive indentation of text shows the supporting and challenging evidence for a solution, and the re-sources supporting evidence (Figure 1).

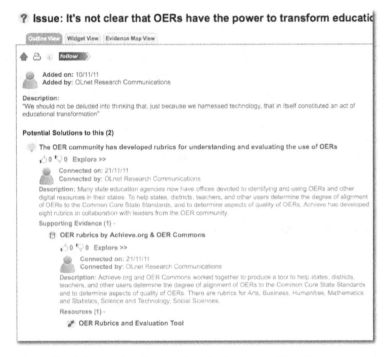

Fig. 1. Linear-threaded Interface for Arguments Visualization

4.4   The Network Interface for Arguments Visualization

The network interface was used by Group 2: This consists of an argument map built by following the modified IBIS, PHI model of arguments [44]. Each statement added to the discussion is here represented as a node in a semantic graph structure (Figure 2). In this visualization, node icons and colors represent the rhetorical role of the statement in the discussion: issues are characterized by a red question mark icon in a dark turquoise node (yellow in Figure 2 because the node is selected); solutions are distinguished by a light bulb icon (see light green nodes), while pro and con are characterized by purple nodes and are connected with a green link or red link to respectively indicate "supporting" or "challenging" relations.

The network visualization of the Evidence Hub is build with a Java Applet, which lays out the nodes dynamically, and following a gravitational algorithm. This adds a specific animation component to most common argument network visualization tools.

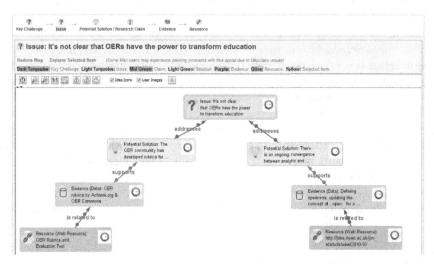

Fig. 2. Screenshot of the Network Interface for Arguments Visualization

5   Data Analysis and Results

The experimentation design aimed to provide an answer to the RQ by focusing on three specific information-seeking tasks (for issues of space we skip detailed description of the tasks):

1. Identifying solutions to an issue (Task1)
2. Identifying synergies between solutions (Task 2)
3. Identifying contrasts in the wider debate (Task 3)

The tasks lasted about 2 to 3 minute and required users to scan 1-3 Webpages (about 1500 - 4000 words) depending on the task.

The three higher-level class of codes emerged from the grounded theory analysis of the user-interaction videos were used as metrics to compare the user's performance across the three tasks. The metrics are: Task Accomplishment; Data Model Interpretation and Emotional Reactions to the two interfaces. From the grounded theory analysis, these metrics have been found to represent the most relevant factors affecting interaction and therefore have been used to assess users' performance with the two interfaces. In the following we analyze and compare users' performance by focusing on each of these metrics and providing users code to motivate our understanding.

5.1   Task Accomplishment

Four main sub-categories of *accomplishment* emerged form the coding: *Accomplished easily, Accomplish but incorrect, Not accomplished*, and *Give Up the task*. From the analysis of the quotations and of the screen capture video of the interaction we found that the main reason of failure was task's understanding. Most interaction events coded as "*Accomplished but incorrect*" were reported in Group 1. The linear structure of the interface is not designed to help interconnecting and comparing content and this has proved to be a burden to the user. As a consequence of this limitation, users who interacted with the linear interface focused more on issues of content's style and validity, rather than on the argumentation process, which lead to digressions and incorrect responses. On the contrary the interaction events coded as "*Accomplished easily*" were mainly experienced in Group 2. This is mainly due to the visual hints provided by the network representation. Specifically, links labels and colours seemed particularly predominant in determining success. We noticed that, the users who *accomplished the task easily* usually relayed on links colours and label, and paid less attention to the iconography of the nodes. The number of links (connections density) also proved to be a very effective way to provide answers to the task.

5.2   Comparing Data Model Interpretation

In order to compare linear and network visualization of arguments in term of how they supported Data Model Interpretation (DMI) we first identified the emerging codes related to DMI and merged them under the following 5 main classes (1. *get the model right, 2. get the categories right, 3. get the model but is unsure, 4. misinterpret categories, 5 does not get the model at all*). We then analysed the interaction events and quotations for each main class.

Results show that DMI was better supported by network visualization of arguments. Category misinterpretation and uncertainty in data model interpretation tend to occur more frequently in Group1 than in Group2, while network visualization of arguments seems to support a complete and correct understanding of both categories and data model. Findings suggest that one possible motivation for this is that argument maps provides examples of how the content of discussion is interpreted in the data model supported by the Evidence hub. In this way users can learn by example ("*let's see what other people have put under this category*" - P8) and at each exploration of a new argument map they reinforce their understanding of the data model ("*this is my solution and this evidence support the solution, and these two nodes challenges it...the clue is the red "challenges" link -P7*)".

5.3   Comparing Emotional Reactions

Emotional reaction to the graphical representation of arguments is another emerg-ing category that we used to measure users satisfaction and emotional attitude toward the two proposed interfaces. Results show that a general sense of surprice and positiv-ity toward the network visualization was recorded, which easily sparks into linkeness and even exhitment (*"ahhh so fabulous!"*-P7; *"wow this is amazing!"*-P6). This postive emotional reaction also seems to be associated to an increase of user' s confidence with the tool (*"I feel confident, I'm pretty sure this is the answer"*-P7). The main object of positivity toward the network visualizations was the self-arranging graph applet. The Applet presents argument maps as floating nodes and edges, slowly moving and arranging on the screen (*"it is like a jelly, it is so fantastic!"*-P7; *"it is all shifting! It is interesting... I quite like that!"*-P8). Movements provoked surprise and excitement and it was also recognized as a useful information feedback. By looking at the floating network, users understood that the map was not static and they could move nodes around and play with it. Users reported that they mostly enjoy this feature. In summary, findings suggest that: moving arranging, zooming and pinning are the network features which most augment users confidence and satisfaction with the tool. On the contrary emotional reactions to the linear interface for arguments visualization were general *skepticism* and *dissatisfaction*, and sometime also decayed to *confusion* and *feeling lost* (*"I think I am lost"*-P1; *"I am now really annoyed.. because I haven't worked   out how to do it" "that is the all page I am looking at?...ohhh ok I give up!"*-P5). Some users explicitly identified the cause of their frustration and said that they needed *"too many clicks"* to seek information and frequent *"change of context"* which often provoked disorientation.

6   Contributions and Future Research

The grounded theory analysis of the experimentation's video showed that different graphical interfaces for the representation of arguments strongly affect the way in which users read and understand the online discourse. Network-like representations and visual hints such as network structure, iconography, links' labels and colors seem to facilitate the identification of argumentation chains, thus supporting indirect connection and higher-level inferences of how the content connects. The results show that data model interpretation is also improved by argument visualization. Notably, exposing the data model in form of argument maps appears to enable learning-by-example mechanisms, whereby users reinforce their understanding of the data as they navigate through the user interface. Finally there is an element of fun and excitement associated to dynamic network visualization of arguments. This may suggest that this type of arguments visualization could be useful for e-participation processes in which the element of "play" and positive emotional reaction are key factors to success. This paper shows promising results on the capability of network visualization of arguments to support reading and sensemaking of online discourse activity. Of course the challenge for e-participation is: how can we move from lab experiments to real world setting and scale the use of CSAV from small group to collectives. Future research will be devoted to explore the use of CSAV and other form of visual analytics to improve users' engagement and sensemaking of large-scale online deliberation processes.

Acknowledgements. The authors thank the support of Catalyst (FP7 program - grant agreement #6111188) under which this work has been finalised.

Reference

1. Shirky, C.: Here Comes Everybody: How change happens when people come together (2009)
2. Sunstein, C.R.: Infotopia: How Many Minds Produce Knowledge. Infotopia: How Many Minds Produce Knowledge (2006)
3. Klein, M., Iandoli, L.: Supporting Collaborative Deliberation Using a Large-Scale Argumentation System: The MIT Collaboratorium (2008)
4. Kunz, W., Rittel, H.W.J.: Issues as elements of information systems (1970)
5. OECD: Promise and Problems of E-Democracy: Challenges of Online Citizen Engagement. 1–162 (2003)
6. Benn, N., Macintosh, A.: Argument Visualization for eParticipation: Towards a Research Agenda and Prototype Tool. In: Tambouris, E., Macintosh, A., de Bruijn, H. (eds.) ePart 2011. LNCS, vol. 6847, pp. 60–73. Springer, Heidelberg (2011)
7. Gordon, T., Macintosh, A., Renton, A.: DEMO-net: D5. 2: Argumentation Support Systems, http://itc.napier.ac.uk
8. Renton, A., Macintosh, A.: Computer-Supported Argument Maps as a Policy Memory. The Information Society 23, 125–133 (2007)
9. Efthimios Tambouris, N.L.A.K.T.: A Framework for Assessing eParticipation Projects and Tools, pp. 1–10 (2006)
10. Buckingham Shum, S.B.: The roots of computer supported argument visualization. Visualizing argumentation (2003)
11. Engelbart, D.C.: Conceptual Framework for the Augmentation of Man\'s Intellect (1963)
12. Novak, J.D.: Learning, creating, and using knowledge: Concept maps as facilitative tools in schools and corporations (2010)
13. Conklin, J., Begeman, M.L.: gIBIS: a hypertext tool for exploratory policy discussion. ACM Trans. Inf. Syst. 6, 303–331 (1988)
14. Horn, R.E.: Visual language and converging technologies in the next 10-15 years (and beyond). In: Proceedings of the 10th WSEAS International Conference on Applied Informatics and Communications (2002)
15. Halasz, F.G., Moran, T.P., Trigg, R.H.: Notecards in a nutshell. Presented at the CHI 1987: Proceedings of the SIGCHI/GI Conference on Human Factors in Computing Systems and Graphics Interface (April 1987)
16. Schuler, W., Smith, J.B.: Author's Argumentation Assistant (AAA): a hypertext-based authoring tool for argumentative texts. Hypertext: concepts, systems and applications (1992)
17. Shipman III, F.M., Marshall, C.C.: Formality Considered Harmful: Experiences, EmergingThemes, and Directions on the Use of Formal Representations inInteractive Systems. Computer Supported Cooperative Work 8 (1999)
18. Fischer, G., Lemke, A.C., McCall, R., Morch, A.I.: Making Argumentation Serve Design. Human-Computer Interaction 6, 393–419 (1991)
19. Buckingham Shum, S., Hammond, N.: Argumentation-based design rationale: what use at what cost? International Journal of Human-Computer Studies 40 (1994)
20. Simon, S., Erduran, S., Osborne, J.: Enhancing the quality of argumentation in school science. Journal of Research in Science Teaching 41(10), 994–1020 (2004)
21. Macintosh, A.: The emergence of digital governance. Significance (2008)
22. Macintosh, A.: E-democracy and e-participation research in Europe. Digital Government (2008)
23. Klein, M.: The MIT Collaboratorium: Enabling Effective Large-Scale Deliberation for Complex Problems (2007)

24. Scheuer, O., Loll, F., Pinkwart, N., McLaren, B.M.: Computer-supported argumentation: A review of the state of the art. International Journal of Computer-Supported Collaborative Learning 5, 43–102 (2010)
25. Suthers, D.D.: Collaborative representations: Supporting face to face and online knowledge-building discourse. System Sciences (2001)
26. Suthers, D., Weiner, A., Connelly, J.: Belvedere: Engaging students in critical discussion of science and public policy issues. In: Proceedings of the 7th World Conference on Artificial Intelligence in Education (1995)
27. De Groot, R., Drachman, R., Hever, R.: CSCL 2007: Proceedings of the 8th Iternational Conference on Computer supported Collaborative Learning (2007)
28. Gordon, T.F., Prakken, H., Walton, D.: The Carneades model of argument and burden of proof. Artificial Intelligence 171 (2007)
29. Van Gelder, T.: The rationale for Rationale™. Law (2007)
30. Bell, P.: Using argument representations to make thinking visible for individuals and groups. Presented at the Proceedings of the 2nd International Conference on Computer Support for Collaborative Learning, Toronto, Ontario, Canada (1997)
31. Linn, M.C., Clark, D., Slotta, J.D.: WISE design for knowledge integration. Sci. Ed. 87, 517–538 (2003)
32. Conklin, J.E.: Conklin: "Designing organizational memory: preserving intellectual assets in a knowledge economy". Group Decision Support Systems 1, 362 (1996)
33. Buckingham Shum, S., Selvin, A.M., Sierhuis, M., Conklin, J., Haley, C.B., Nuseibeh, B.: Hypermedia Support for Argumentation-Based Rationale. Presented at the, Berlin, Heidelberg (2006)
34. De Liddo, A., Buckingham Shum, S., Convertino, G., Sándor, Á., Klein, M.: Collective intelligence as community discourse and action. Presented at the CSCW 2012: Proceedings of the ACM 2012 Conference on Computer Supported Cooperative Work Companion (February 2012)
35. Buckingham Shum, S.: Cohere: Towards Web 2.0 Argumentation. Presented at the Proceeding of the 2008 Conference on Computational Models of Argument: Proceedings of COMMA 2008 (June 2008)
36. Rahwan, I., Zablith, F., Reed, C.: Laying the foundations for a world wide argument web. Artificial Intelligence (2007)
37. MacLean, A., Young, R.M., Bellotti, V.M.E., Moran, T.P.: Questions, options, and criteria: elements of design space analysis. Human-Computer Interaction 6 (1991)
38. Karacapilidis, N., Tzagarakis, M., Karousos, N.: Tackling cognitively-complex collaboration with CoPe_it! International Journal of Web-Based Learning and Teaching Technologies (IJWLTT) 4(3), 22–38 (2009)
39. Hair, D.C.: LEGALESE: a legal argumentation tool. SIGCHI Bulletin 23 (1991)
40. Hill, W.C., Hollan, J.D., Wroblewski, D., McCandless, T.: Edit wear and read wear. Presented at the CHI 1992: Proceedings of the SIGCHI Conference on Human Factors in Computing Systems (June 1992)
41. Glaser, B.G., Strauss, A.L., Strutzel, E.: The discovery of grounded theory; strategies for qualitative research. Nursing Research (1968)
42. Brown, E., Cairns, P.: A grounded investigation of game immersion. In: CHI 2004 extended Abstracts on Human Factors in Computing Systems. ACM (2004)
43. De Liddo, A., Buckingham Shum, S.: The Evidence Hub: harnessing the collective intelligence of communities to build evidence-based knowledge (2013)
44. McCall, R.J.: PHI: A conceptual foundation for design hypermedia. Design Studies (1991)

Engaging Citizens in Policy Issues: Multidimensional Approach, Evidence and Lessons Learned

Elena Sánchez-Nielsen[1], Deirdre Lee[2], Eleni Panopoulou[3], Simon Delakorda[4], and Gyula Takács[5]

[1] Departmento de Ingeniería Informática, Universidad de La Laguna, S/C de Tenerife, Spain
[2] DERI, NUI Galway, IDA Business Park, Lower Dangan, Ireland
[3] Centre for R&T Hellas (CERTH) and Greek R&T Network (GRNET), Greece
[4] Institute for Electronic Participation (INePA), Ljubljana, Slovenia
[5] NISZ National Infocommunications Service Compay Ltd., Hungary
enielsen@ull.edu.es, Deirdre.Lee@deri.org, epanopou@iti.gr, Simon.delakorda@inepa.si, takacs.gyulapeter@nisz.hu

Abstract. E-participation offers individuals, groups and non-governmental institutions the opportunity to learn about and discuss policy so they can make more informed choices in their personal lives as citizens, and to contribute to policy drafting as an instrument to strengthen the quality of decision-makers' actions. Although a growing body of literature has been devoted to the main benefits and opportunities that ICT can offer in e-participation, little is known about the driving forces that foster public participation and citizens' active engagement. This paper describes a multidimensional engagement approach, supported by an inform-consult-empower framework, to strengthen the foundation for participatory policy-making. This approach addresses the following key issues: public participation, public involvement, deliberative democracy, and collaborative governance. This approach has been designed, investigated and applied in the context of the European Commission project "Puzzled by Policy: Helping you be part of the EU". The findings suggest that the use of a multidimensional engagement approach with a user-centric focus from the outset is essential to foster social participation, raise trust between citizens and government, and promote constructive narratives to put into the policy-making process.

1   Introduction

Active citizen engagement and clear impact are hallmarks of a successful e-participation initiative. In recent years, the EU and its Member States have mounted a concerted effort to find workable mechanisms to enhance e-participation under the Fifth, Sixth and Seventh Framework Programmes for Research. This was continued under the CIP ICT Policy Support Programme in 2009, which focused on empowering and involving citizens in transparent decision making [1]. Many of these e-participation projects have not been as successful as initially anticipated [2]. This is somewhat surprising, as many studies have shown that there are many benefits of

E. Tambouris et al. (Eds.): ePart 2014, LNCS 8654, pp. 102–113, 2014.

citizen participation, including tapping into local knowledge and innovation, reducing or avoiding conflict, increasing social inclusion or cohesion, mobilising new resources including voluntary labour, reducing transaction costs, and generating trust and social capital [3]. In this context, one of the main lessons identified by the 2009 European e-participation Summary Report is that more focus is needed on better e-participation project design [4]. The key dimensions to characterize e-participation initiatives have been described by Macintosh [5] and the OECD Report [6]. Recently, the importance of including social media political discussions between citizens in e-participation platforms has also been outlined [7]. Although a growing body of literature has been devoted to the main benefits and opportunities that ICT can offer in e-participation, little is known about the driving forces that foster public participation and citizens' active participation. Therefore, a lot of lessons still have to be learned about how to use ICT effectively for public engagement in e-participation initiatives.

The aim of this paper is to argue that citizens cannot be viewed just as a digital audience to politics or merely as virtual customers of government. Instead, citizens should be treated as a vital resource for effective problem solving and community building to offer a plausible solution to policy-making challenges. With this goal, an inform-consult-empower theoretical framework developed in earlier work [8, 12] is used to identify the core dimensions we propose are vital to overcome the challenges of engagement from the perspective of an e-participation initiative.

The remainder of this paper is organized as follows. Section 2 reviews the state of practice of citizen engagement. Section 3 outlines the inform-consult-empower theoretical framework that is used to support the proposed multidimensional engagement approach and the Puzzled by Policy platform that is used to test this approach. Section 4 describes the rationale and key dimensions of the engagement approach. Section 5 provides the evidence to date with the use of this engagement approach in the Puzzled by Policy project. Section 6 gives lessons learned of interest to anyone who is trying to use ICT in order to support online democratic engagement. Finally, section 7 points out the main conclusions.

2   State of Practice of Citizen Engagement

Democracies around the world face challenges related to citizen engagement with political institutions. Discussions theoretically allow citizens to air their disagreements, create opportunities to reconsider initial approaches, and foster understanding of alternative perspective and viewpoints [9]. In recent years, traditional approaches to connect citizens with decision-makers and policy-making have evolved. There has been a shift from citizens as passive consumers to active participants in the policy-making process. This adjustment towards viewing citizen engagement as fundamental knowledge-building contributes to the transparency, legitimacy and fairness of policy development. However, simply opening up a policy-making process to citizens is not sufficient to ensure public engagement. Currently, there are diverse reasons for citizens and decision makers to not become involved in the policy making process. On the citizen side, two broad groups can be identified [10]: audiences who are 'willing but unable' to participate due to a variety of reasons such as cultural or language barriers, geographical distance, disability, or socio-economic status reflecting in digital inequalities (divide), and audiences who are 'able but unwilling' to participate, perhaps because they are not very interested in politics, do not have the time, or do not trust government to make good use of their input. In order to ensure the engagement of these types of hard-to-reach audiences, as well as the general public, it is vital to design a holistic public engagement approach. While the use of ICT approaches can certainly help with accessibility, transparency, dissemination and analysis, they should not be viewed as a complete solution.

To date, a lot of common approaches to public engagement in decision processes reflect a mechanistic, top-down orientation that does not maximize the benefits of public engagement [15, 16]. Policy-makers with a particular goal or domain in mind initiate a discussion and try and encourage people to contribute. This kind of participation is important as those with the power to implement the results of the discussion are directly involved. The challenges of such initiatives are sometimes seen by the public as fake engagements, with no real potential for impact. Or the impact of the discussion is diluted in the political process and its effects are not clear for those participating. As a consequence, bottom-up approaches and grassroots movements have alternatively risen in recent years. As an organic development of ideas, this approach to participation can introduce topics onto the agenda that the policy-makers may not have originally been interested in. On the other side, bottom-up movements may find it difficult to have any impact until at some stage the policy-makers pay attention and engage in discussions. Therefore, these types of initiatives need a critical mass behind it as well as organisational capacities.

3   Puzzled by Policy Concept

Puzzled by Policy aims to reduce the complexity of decision making within the EU and reconnect citizens with decision makers and policy making in an engaging way. Puzzled by Policy is modelled around an inform-consult-empower framework designed in previous work [8, 12] which offers all stakeholders the opportunity to participate in an appropriate and achievable setting based on the stage of the policy process they are. The aim is to offer different levels of participation that is realistic and achievable. Inform-consult-empower framework recognises that citizen engagement is an iterative process; initially people are more likely to want to simply find out information about policies than to discuss them; subsequently, people are more inclined to discuss policy topics than to propose new ideas or drive policy change. The inform-consult-empower framework is structured in terms of Kingdon's Multiple Stream Model [11] and the Conference of International NGOs of the Council of Europe's Policy Cycle Model [17]. Both models are complementary, representing sequential phases of the policy-making process. The multiple stream model represents the topical discussion, lobbying and proposing that takes place on an ongoing basis. Once a policy window appears, i.e. a problem has been defined, a solution has been identified and the political conditions are right, the policy decision-making cycle comes into effect. The combined model recognises that although decision-makers may or may not play a role in the problem stream and policy stream during phase 1, they must be involved in order for a policy window to appear and phase 2 to come into effect. To facilitate online democratic engagement, the Puzzled by Policy Platform[1] was developed supported on this inform-consult-empower framework. This platform consists of three components, which have initially been designed around immigration policy, but can be applied to any policy domain. The Policy Profiler is a Web based tool which gives users the opportunity to find out about their preferences within the policy field of immigration. Furthermore, it allows users to compare their positions to the existing policy framework. U-debate is a multilingual, pan-European deliberation forum where users can view, discuss and share ideas on immigration policy. The goal of U-debate is to create consultation reports on policy topics, relating to draft policies or topics of public concern at local, national or EU level. In particular, the Puzzled by Policy U-debate tool is focused on the use of a deliberation model. The Widget enables the viral distribution of the Puzzled by Policy Platform throughout the Web, as the Widget can be embedded, and thus accessed, on any website, blog or social media site on the Internet.

4 Multidimensional Engagement Approach

Section 2 described the main challenges of incorporating citizen engagement into e-participation initiatives. This section lays out a 13-dimension engagement approach that harnesses innovative technologies in cross-border and multilevel democratic decision-making. Although research and evidence have shown that there is no "one-size-fits-all" solution to involve citizens in policy making, there are essential dimensions that should be addressed in order to design a successful approach. The engagement approach presented in this paper is supported by an inform-consult-empower framework developed in earlier work [8, 12], developed in consultation with academics and experts on e-participation, and based on a review of several existing frameworks that have been created around the world [5, 9, 11, 15] in order to address the following requirements of e-participation initiatives [16]: how to attract and sustain citizen participation, how to foster public involvement, how to promote deliberative democracy, and how to induce collaborative government. We found that to maximize the impact of e-participation programmes, these are the main elements that have to be defined when planning the pilot trials that use ICT:

1. **Purposes and Objectives:** Before launching an e-participation initiative, it is critical: to decide to what extent you are committed to taking public opinion into account in your decision making and to communicate clearly the nature of that commitment. The objectives have to be concrete, realistic, engaging and effective. As a consequence, it is essential to ensure the trust in the quality of what the public can contribute to the policy-making process.
2. **Strategy:** Implementing real-world settings for active citizen engagement requires a detailed operation and dissemination plan. Operation strategy

---

[1] http://join.puzzledbypolicy.eu/

encompasses the definition of topics and policy processes, identification of target groups and stakeholders, developing, testing and launching online tools, management and, facilitation. The dissemination plan addresses the dissemination strategy and channels for strategic promotion and marketing to engage users.

3. **Process Set up:** Setting up an e-participation initiative consists of defining a communication space where interactions among participants are taking place and content is produced and shared. It is not necessarily limited to policy-making and can also focus on societal participation or community building. E-participation initiatives present their main communication space through the use of online tools and can be extended by face-to-face communication and online social media. In order to establish a trustworthy and efficient communication space, it is essential to define communication norms that enable participants to engage into civilized interaction.

4. **Management:** Management of ICTs in cross-border and multilevel democratic-decision-making includes the following key elements: coordinating implementation activities, monitoring overall performance, ensuring goals and success criteria are met, managing risks and administering leads.

5. **Topic Selection:** Topic selection encompasses aspects like setting up a contextual framework for the information and the consultation level of participation. The main goal of topic selection is background information published on policy issues including data on policy developments, legislation, stakeholders' positions, public opinion, historical and institutional framework. As this content is usually very complex and information rich, topic presentation has to be extracted in an engaging and meaningful way for participants to read and understand.

6. **Target Group Identification:** The overall performance of an e-participation initiative in democratic decision-making and engaging participants depends on the adequate identification and involvement of target groups and stakeholders. There are three major target groups of potential users in selected policy field or public affairs: (1) decision-makers (government officials and politicians), (2) civil society professionals and volunteers (academia, experts, non-governmental organizations, media, labour unions, enterprises, informal groups, individual citizens) and (3) every-day-citizens: practising active citizenship. Any successful engagement approach design requires trade-offs between the intensity of small groups and the representativeness of larger samples. Local voluntary groups as leader groups are crucial to creating awareness and drawing average citizens into dialogue about their communities. These groups can act as intermediaries between the individual and decision-makers.

7. **Time Frame:** Planning time frames is essential to engage target audiences in a successful way. It is related to initiative duration and relevance. The impact of using ICTs for democratic decision-making is often depending on whether a topic or an issue addressed is currently on the political, public or media agenda. Therefore, e-participation initiative operation duration has to correlate to relevant public or political processes (e.g. public consultations), events (e.g. elections) and developments (e.g. economic crisis). Relevance time frames can be different in duration, comparing to operation time frames. As a consequence, participation initiatives have to be flexible by following up with developments in the field and respond to them, when there is an opportunity to influence policy-making.

8. **ICT Tools:** Combining different online tools can help reducing the complexity of decision making. Tools developed should be designed in order to support different levels of participation when an inform-consult-empower framework is used [5, 8, 12], as well as, to address the needs and characteristics of diverse target groups. ICT tools design should combine elements of user-friendliness, visual appeals, and simplicity. A web site encompassing ICT tools selection by providing additional information about the initiative, community, developments, and results helps foster public involvement. Social media profiles and viral distribution can also facilitate community building. Allowing participants to co-design ICT tools can help involve them in the actual use of these tools.

9. **Facilitation and Support for Deliberative Democracy:** Facilitation is required when an e-participation initiative features interactive online and offline discussions and consultations, aiming to deliver policy related content. On the other hand, hard-to-reach target groups (less educated, elderly, etc.) sometimes do not have adequate know-how or resources to fully benefit from the online tools available. Therefore, providing support channels for user inclusion is required. Moreover, the use of social deliberative skills is also essential for a successful facilitation. These skills refer to the abilities that participants need in order to work toward mutual understanding, mutual regard, and trust in deliberations in which participants start with heterogeneous goals, assumptions, values, or world-views. A non-active use of social deliberative skills lead to several inefficiencies: (1) some comments do not mesh with the topic to be discussed, and (2) use of the platform to discuss personal stories rather than the ideas presented. On the other hand, the use of negative language based on problems and criticism invites participants to focus on the negative aspects of individuals or communities, triggering defensiveness and as a result, tends to discredit or belittle [13]. The use of social deliberative approaches conceived to foster a collaborative construction of reality based on a systematic search for what works best is a key way to achieve a positive community and deliberative response [14].

10. **Dissemination and Involvement:** Regular and intensive dissemination is fundamental to create public visibility of the project. Dissemination should cover the online platform and its tools, share results, raise awareness in general, and also reach out to specific target groups. In general, a two-step planning is necessary to reach public visibility. The first step consists of identifying generic (mass media, TV, press, radio, etc.) and specific (web sites, blogs, social media, networks, etc.) dissemination channels related to the policy issue, as well as creating new channels for the initiative (web site, e-mail, Facebook, Twitter, LinkedIn, Flickr and YouTube profiles). The second step focuses on creating professional and consistent dissemination materials (brand/logo, posters, web banners, bookmarks, initiative brochure and video presentation), which present key messages (teasers). Dissemination activities should include viral marketing, e-mailing, phone calls, newsletters and press releases, meetings, interviews, discussions, demonstrations, focus groups, workshops for target groups, conferences, online articles, and also participating at events related to the policy-issue of the participation initiative.

11. **Feedback and Impact:** The first step to induce collaborative governance and successful engagement is a strong commitment to receive decision-makers' feedback and to create an impact analysis. Feedback and impact provide concrete evidence on how target groups' and stakeholders' input (e.g. citizen's opinions and positions) is considered by decision-makers, and how it is influencing policy-making (empower level of participation). At the same time, it generates trust in political institutions due to transparency of the process, as well perceiving participation initiatives as a viable tool for contributing to better decision-making.

12. **Monitoring and Evaluation:** In essence, evaluation is the process of bringing all the e-participation initiative's results together to determine project success, impact achieved, lessons learned and to propose further recommendations and best practice. Statistical and qualitative information should be monitored on regular basis to keep on track with platform operation and to undertake timely actions for addressing potential risks. Evaluation serves several purposes such as: (1) to evaluate the results of the initiative; (2) to assess usefulness to citizens and decision makers, (3) to identify best practices; and (4) to provide further technical refinement suggestions, particularly with regard to accessibility and sustainability, and recommendations for correctly using the platform.

13. **Sustainability:** It is important to ensure that initiative results are available for an easy and cost-effective replication by potential adopters. A lot of e-participation trials in Europe are facing sustainability issues, therefore it is important to ensure that the technical solutions developed, as well as the experience and knowledge generated, will be utilized and sustained after the official project lifecycle has ended. The development of sustainability toolkits material is essential to enable potential adopters to explore the benefits of the participation initiative.

5   Evidence to Date

Puzzled by Policy kicked off in October 2010 with the aim of engaging citizens in the policy-making process. It was piloted in real-world settings across Greece, Hungary, Italy, and Spain. The purpose of the pilots was to engage key national and EU stakeholders into the e-participation process, covering immigration-policy issues by providing information, content management, process facilitation and promotion of the Puzzled by Policy platform, and to deliver policy proposals for targeted decision-makers and institutions. A feedback mechanism for delivering results to the key decision makers via the tool and/or report was established, so recommendations could be made on how to shape/implement the immigration proposals that provide the most positive policy impacts to all involved. The use of the multidimensional approach described in section 4 resulted in significant engagement and the Puzzled by Policy platform proved very successful during 15 months of pilot operation, with 212,700 page views and 17,000 unique visitors. Over 6,800 people actively participated on the pilots, meaning that they at least completed the Policy Profiler quiz. In relation to the involvement of stakeholders, more than 100 NGOs were involved and over ten policy-makers at local, regional, and national levels. More than 1300 contributions were published in 118 u-debate discussions threads by 600 users. Eight informal and six formal feedbacks have been received from decision-makers. Table 1 summarizes the key points of this multidimensional approach in Puzzled by Policy project.

Table 1. Summary of key dimensions and outcomes in the Puzzled by Policy project

Dimensions	Outcomes
Purposes and objectives	Focus on irregular immigration to support social care services in Greece. Identification of immigration and emigration issues by users, policy makers and NGOs in Hungary. Discussing key policy topics on local election entitlement to vote, citizenship, and qualification and professionalism acknowledgement in Italy. And, strengthening social participation to incite urban dwellers and decision makers to participate in shaping migration policies in Spain.
Strategy	All pilot countries were a great example of grass-roots, bottom-up citizens' discussions that blend online and face-to-face activities to shape immigration issues and topics.
Process set up	Focus on policy-making, societal participation, and community building. Multilingualism was enabled by offering the platform interface in the four pilot languages besides English, and by an automatic translation tool to make user generated debate content accessible in all major languages.
Management	Constant and flexible management by pilots. Creation of feedback channels with decision-makers.
Topics selection	14 topic statements were identified in the fields of immigration for employment purposes, immigration for studying purposes, immigration for reasons of family reunification, long-term resident immigration, and irregular immigration. Enabling bottom-up identification of topics by NGOs, advocacy groups and individuals was further strengthening inclusiveness of the process, and motivating decision-makers, stakeholders and participants to recognize and use Puzzled by Policy online platform as a relevant channel for participation.
Target groups	Hard-to-reach group of pilot trials was defined as being under-represented in immigration policy-making due to limited access and knowledge about decision-making, or due to low level of ICTs skills. This group was composed of immigrant, young, elderly, less educated and unemployed people.
Time frame	Pilot countries were flexible by following with up-to-date developments and responsive to act, when there was an opportunity to influence policy-making in terms of adopting 'hot' topics.
ICT tools	The web site www.puzzledbypolicy was encompassing ICT tools selection by providing additional information about the project, community, developments and results.
Deliberative democracy	An appreciative inquiry model [13] was explored and applied by the Spanish pilot in order to foster and vitalize the active engagement of the different actors involved in online and offline debates. The use of this approach has shown that it was the questions designed from an appreciative approach that yielded the most visits and comments
Dissemination	Multichannel and multilingual dissemination at the national and the EU level was supported by a news agency partner. Face-to-face dissemination and looking for synergies with immigration mediators in the field, who had already established communication channels, provided additional visibility for pilot countries.
Feedback	Official feedbacks received from decision-makers were disseminated through pilot countries' dissemination channels, and a special sub-page was established within the platform that provided access to pilot countries' consultation reports and feedbacks received from decision-makers, to induce collaborative governance on how to shape/implement the immigration proposals that provide the most beneficial policy impacts to all involved.
Monitoring and evaluation	A five-pillar framework was used to evaluate the project. These pillars were: evaluation metrics, evaluation stakeholders, evaluation instruments, and data collection tools and data analysis tools. An impact analysis was performed by developing an impact table referring to each level of the inform-consult-empower framework, and an analytical framework referring to different components such as: external factors, resources, operational results, and quantitative, qualitative, political, societal and cultural outcomes.
Sustainability	A sustainability toolkit was developed to enable potential adopters to explore the benefits of Puzzled by Policy, hosted by a standalone web site (http://puzzledbypolicy.moonfruit.com/).

6   Lessons Learned

Addressing public engagement is a critical challenge for the design, development, and implementation policy in the 21st century. Reaching out to target groups requires huge effort, commitment, and funding. In addition to the costs of suitable technology, these e-participation projects require careful planning and consistent facilitation and moderation. Through the implementation of the aforementioned dimensions, we have drawn key lessons learned from the Puzzled by Policy pilots. These can be summarized as:

1. **The Initiative Owner Should Embrace Users and have a User-Centric Attitude:** Users' needs and expectations from tangible (platform and tools) and intangible (the participatory process) aspects should be taken under consideration throughout the initiative. Engaging citizens in policy-making is not a means for diminishing representation, but for strengthening it. Identification of relevant topics should be implemented in bottom-up collaboration with target (interest) groups, experts, and decision-makers. Complex topics need to be presented in a simple yet relevant way aided by starting questions, data visualisations, or scenario building, enabling participants to provide different kinds of inputs (opinions, proposals, arguments, etc.). Sensitive topics should be addressed by mediators in the policy field and by allowing anonymous participation supported by active facilitation. However, anonymity provides room for inappropriate comments and insults, while identification typically leads to a more constructive conversation online.

2. **Partnership with Mediators in the Policy Field:** Top down oriented projects are facing difficulties in engaging target groups in participatory processes. Project partnership in topics identification, e-participation initiative operation and influencing decision-makers with mediators in the policy field such as civil society organisations, non-governmental organisations, public services and informal groups can increase participation of individuals and communities otherwise not involved in the process. Also, mediators are often acting as stakeholders in the field, actively promoting and increasing participation of target groups via their communication channels and transferring knowledge, experience and feedback. For that purpose, it is essential to network and establish trust with mediators in the policy field. As a result, the bottom-up approach is often more suitable when aiming at a critical mass of participating citizens or when the agenda is not predetermined.

3. **Multichannel Involvement and Wide, Consistent Dissemination is Necessary to Raise Awareness:** Combining advantages of face-to-face group events and the web can result in simultaneous engagement of dispersed groups as well as hard-to-reach individuals having different communication needs and styles. It is also important to maintain a steady dissemination of regular updates on and progress of the participatory process. On the other hand, intensive dissemination campaign such as project or platform launch with a 'bang', are crucial for obtaining an initial visibility of the process. Dissemination content and tool needs to be visually

attractive and user friendly. It is very difficult and demanding to build up a sustainable community of stakeholders around a top-down oriented initiative with a limited time span. Alternatively, it is worth considering a participatory design approach, enabling target groups to identify or even create their own channels of involvement and dissemination suitable to their needs.

4. **Policy Content Production:** High-quality content produced and shaped in a vibrant, multi-stakeholder, open, and trustworthy space and supported by ICT is presenting one of the main foci of smart governance. Generating relevant policy knowledge and information in a structured, detailed and proposal oriented format supported by arguments and evidence, is providing a valuable decision-making resource in addition to the regular public opinion polls. On the other hand, high-quality content provided by an informed and consulted public is enabling policy-makers to make decisions based on relevant and useful information as well as motivating them to participate in the process by providing feedback. Finally, high-quality policy content is attracting the attention of mass media interested to report on publicly relevant topics.

5. **Process Management and Facilitation:** The primary purpose of e-participation management is to enable a successful and transparent implementation of the participatory process. Therefore, well defined goals and expected results (e.g. what will happen with citizen input) are set up in an e-participation implementation plan and a dissemination/involvement plan. Management must also include monitoring the progress and assessing the results/impact of the process (e.g. informed citizens, improved dialogue, and better legislation). Management efforts pursue the sustainability of participatory processes. As a result, adequate organisational and administrative capacity is fundamental when enabling citizen involvement in multilevel and cross-border governance. On the other hand, a primary goal of e-participation facilitation is to establish mutual trust among stakeholders involved and to contribute to the legitimacy of the process. Facilitation is about uncovering hidden agendas and securing equal and unbiased conditions for participation of stakeholders by providing support and guidance. Efforts may include a more or less pro-active mediation (or migration) of views expressed elsewhere, either manually or by using semantic technologies, e.g. by carefully analysing and reposting the core of messages found in social media, in a way that matches the context and structure of the actual consultation. Facilitation is further strengthening transparency of the process by increasing visibility of contributions, creating publicly available summary reports, as well as publishing feedback from decision-makers. In other words, facilitation is bridging easy-to-add contributions and easy-to-absorb summaries Rules of facilitation need to be public. Another key aspect of facilitation is to motivate stakeholders to actively participate in the process and to provide solutions, when there is a stalemate in the process due to conflict.

6. **Decision-Maker Involvement:** Politicians, political parties and government institutions at national and EU level are facing low levels of legitimacy and trust due to quick, unsuccessful, and often unpopular decision-making targeting the social and economic crisis in Europe. As a result, citizens are often not motivated to collaborate with elected officials. Still, it is crucial to identify and engage

trustworthy/accountable politicians to act as stakeholders of participatory projects. An active campaign to engage decision makers in the process of consultation with citizens is needed. Politicians involved need to be active in policy topics which are subject of participatory projects, and they need to have adequate capacities to provide their own input/feedback. Usually, local decision-makers are more flexible to obtain the commitment and involvement of political representatives in order to take into account the proposals which have been built together with stakeholders.

7. **Feedback and Impact:** Receiving decision-makers' formal or informal feedback to pilot' reports (results) during or after the involvement process enables participants and other stakeholders to assess their impact on decision-making. Feedbacks also reflect the actual degree of institutionalized empowerment and relevance of the process. In order to provide feedback, government institutions and politicians have to be informed about topics and engaged in the process from the beginning. For that purpose, facilitator's reports and conclusions deriving from participants' contributions have to be well structured, meaningful and concrete. Since public participation is demanding in terms of time and resources, participants have to be well informed about the impact of involvement and have to have an opportunity to assess how they are benefiting from the process. As a result, actual empowerment is not only political but also societal in nature (e.g. participatory culture, improved communication, community building). Therefore it is very important that decision-makers' feedback and impact evidence are made as public as possible through various dissemination channels in order to induce a collaborative governance.

7   Conclusions

Puzzled by Policy has been an innovative and influential project, pushing boundaries of online citizen engagement on key policy-topics. It has proven to be an adaptive and integrated approach to e-participation, which has set new benchmarks for online participation in the future. Puzzled by Policy uses a multidimensional engagement approach, supported by an inform-consult-empower framework. To maximise the impact of the e-participation process, we defined 13 key dimensions for that have to be defined when planning pilot trials for the purpose of using ICT in cross-border and multilevel democratic decision-making. Puzzled by Policy pilot trials were implemented according to these step-by-step planning, development, implementation, and operation dimensions, which in turn enabled us to extract key lessons learned. The importance of inclusiveness, communication and multichannel were all highlighted in our findings. The results of Puzzled by Policy are embedded in each of the four pilot sites, disseminated throughout the communities and organizations who have now come to expect engagement on policy matters with the official representatives. The Puzzled by Policy approach and platform will be applied to new initiatives, policy-areas and jurisdictions to enable future engagement of citizens on critical policy topics.

Acknowledgements. The work presented in this paper has been funded by the European Union under Grant N° 256261 (Puzzled by Policy – CIP-ICT-PSP-2009-3bis), in part by a research grant from Science Foundation Ireland (SFI) under Grant Number SFI/12/RC/2289", and in part by the Spanish Government under the project TIN2011-24598.

References

1. Europe's Information Society Thematic Portal,
   `http://ec.europa.eu/information_society/activities/ict_psp/`
   `participating/calls/call_proposals_09_bis/index_en.htm`
2. Prieto-Martín, P., de Marcos, L., Martínez, J.: The e-(R)evolution will not be funded. European Journal of ePractice vol. 15: Policy lessons from a decade of eGovernment, eHealth & eInclusion (2012)
3. Smith, S.: D1.3c: Main benefits of eParticipation developments in the EU a contextualisation with reference to the EU governance regime and the European public sphere. In: European eParticipation (ed.) Study and supply of services on the development of eParticipation in the EU (2009)
4. European eParticipation Summary Report (2009),
   `http://ec.europa.eu/information_society/activities/egovernme`
   `nt/docs/reports/eu_eparticipation_summary_nov_09.pdf`
5. Macintosh, A.: Characterizing E-Participation in Policy-Making. In: HICSS 37th (2004)
6. OECD. Promises and problems of e-democracy; Challenges of Citizen on-line Engagement (2003)
7. Porwol, L., Ojo, A., Breslin, J.: Harnessing the duality of e-Participation – Social Software Infraestructure Design. In: ICEGOV (2013)
8. Lee, D., Loutas, N., Sánchez-Nielsen, E., Mogulkoc, E., Lacigova, O.: Inform-consult-empower: A three-tiered approach to eParticipation. In: Tambouris, E., Macintosh, A., de Bruijn, H. (eds.) ePart 2011. LNCS, vol. 6847, pp. 121–132. Springer, Heidelberg (2011)
9. Price, V.: Citizens Deliberation Online: Theory and Some Evidence. In: Davies, T., Gangadharan, S.P. (eds.) Online Deliberation: Design, Research, and Practice, pp. 37–58. CSLI Publications (2009)
10. OECD. Focus on Citizens: Public Engagement for Better Policy and Services, OECD Studies on Public Engagement (2009)
11. Kingdon, "Agendas, Alternatives and Public Policies". Addison-Wesley Publishers (1984)
12. Sánchez-Nielsen, E., Lee, D.: eParticipation in Practice in Europe: The Case of" Puzzled by Policy: Helping You Be Part of EU. In: 46th International Conference on System Sciences (HICSS 2013), pp. 1870–1879. Hawaii, EEUU (2013)
13. Gergen, K.: An invitation to social construction. SAGE Publications, London
14. Sánchez-Nielsen, E., Martín-Váquez, C.: Exploring how the appreciative inquiry model can vitalize the online citizen debate. In: 13th European Conference on e-Government, Como, Italy, pp. 424–431 (2013)
15. Bittle, S., Haller, C., Kadlec, A.: Promising practices in online engagement. Center for Avances in Public Engagement (2009)
16. Shane, P.M. (ed.): Center for Intedisciplinary Law and Policy Studies of the Ohio State University. Building democracy through online citizen deliberation: a framework for action (2008)
17. Conference of International NGO at the Council of Europe 2009. Code of good practice for civil participation in the decision-making process (2009)

A Goal Matching Service for Facilitating Public Collaboration Using Linked Open Data

Shun Shiramatsu[1], Teemu Tossavainen[1,2], Tadachika Ozono[1], and Toramatsu Shintani[1]

[1] Graduate School of Engineering, Nagoya Institute of Technology, Japan
{siramatu,ozono,tora}@nitech.ac.jp
[2] School of Science, Aalto University, Finland
teemu.tossavainen@aalto.fi

Abstract. Inter-organizational collaboration in the public sphere is essentially important to address sustainability problems in contemporary regional societies. To facilitate public collaboration, we are developing a Web application for sharing public issues and their solutions as public goals. Since participating in abstract or general goals is more difficult than concrete or specific ones, our system provides a functionality to break down individual public goals into concrete subgoals. Our Web application, GoalShare, is based on a linked open dataset of public goals that are linked with titles, participants, subgoals, related issues, related articles, and related geographic regions. GoalShare recommends public goals and users on the basis of similarity calculations taking into account not only surficial and semantic features but also contextual features extracted from subgoals and supergoals. We conducted experiments to investigate the effects of contextual features in subgoals and supergoals. Moreover, we conducted a trial workshop with GoalShare in Ogaki city to improve system design through actual use.

Keywords: linked data, civic tech, public involvement, concern assessment, text mining.

1   Introduction

Contemporary human societies confront problems with sustainability, e.g., increased consumption of resources, polarization into rich and poor [1], and catastrophic risks of the disasters due to climate change [2]. Inter-organizational collaboration in the public sphere is essentially important to improve the sustainability of regional society because the sustainability problems are relevant to various stakeholders and are intricately interrelated. There have recently been public collaborations with social networking services (SNSs) to address regional issues in Japan, especially after the Great East Japan Earthquake in 2011 [3,4]. It is, however, difficult to find potential collaborators who have similar public concerns with SNSs because most SNSs emphasize the aspect of real-time information sharing and lack of functions to share "who are trying to address

E. Tambouris et al. (Eds.): ePart 2014, LNCS 8654, pp. 114–127, 2014.

particular issues and what kinds of approaches they take". When many groups focus on similar social issues, collaboration among them reduces nonproductive conflicts and facilitates constructive consensus-building or social innovation.

We have designed linked open data (LOD) of social issues and their solutions as public goals, which enabled us to calculate similarities between public goals [5]. Moreover, we have implemented a prototype of a Web application, called GoalShare (ゴォルシェア   in Japanese), to match citizens or groups who have similar goals to facilitate public collaboration and open innovation [6]. For this purpose, user-generated LOD of public goals are linked with personal identifiers of existing SNSs and geographical identifiers of existing geographical LODsets by the GoalShare system. In this paper, we discuss its applicability to public collaboration in the real world and empirical investigations based on an actual dataset of public goals gathered in Japanese regional societies.

The matching function needs to take into consideration two conditions to inter-organizationally match people with their collaboration potential.

(a) Similarity of issues focused on or goals aimed at.

(b) Complementarity of required skills, abilities, or resources.

This paper especially focuses on condition (a) as a first step. Matching with condition (b) can be formulated as a two-sided matching problem that is often modeled on the basis of the game theory [7]. We do not limit the matching function to two-sided matching because many citizens, who have similar aims like those in condition (a), can be candidate collaborators one after another in the process of solving social issues.

We designed a hierarchical data model for goal description to break down an abstract goal into concrete subgoals in our previous studies [5]. Our data model could be regarded as a simplification of a prerequisite tree (PRT) in the theory of constraint (TOC) pioneered by Goldratt [8]. Data on issues and goals are linked in our model with personal information such as participants, with geographical information such as related regions, and with temporal information such as deadlines to specialize them in public participation. We expect three effects by sharing LOD in a hierarchical goal structure.

(i) Providing Hints As To Which Activity can be Contributed To. It is difficult to determine how to participate in or contribute to an abstract or general goal, whereas it is easier to determine whether a concrete subgoal can be contributed to or not because the grain-size of concrete subgoals is closer to actual actions or activities than that of abstract goals.

(ii) Sharing Context for Negotiations of Collaboration Among Groups. Even groups that have similar objectives occasionally conflict with one another because subgoals are sometimes difficult to be agreed on even if the final goal is generally agreed on. Visualizing their goal hierarchies enables them to compare the structures, to check which part is conflictive, and to try to find a common ground.

(iii) **Sophisticating Calculations of Similarities between Goals.** To calculate similarities, the hierarchical structure enables us to use not only surficial or semantic features in textual goal descriptions but also contextual features such as supergoals or subgoals.

Although the hierarchical structure of goals needs to be input through deliberative processes, we need to gather public goals and issues from regional societies at the early stages of service operation. We assumed three ways of inputting public goals at an early stage.

(1) **Input by Goal Owners.** Identical people who have goals personally input and publish them to disclose their own activities and explore potential collaborators.

(2) **Input by Interviewers.** Researchers, social workers, or government officers ask citizens about issues and input their responses. They also create solutions as goal data and find potential contributors.

(3) **Input by Third Parties Using References.** Citizens extract public goals planned by key personalities from fragmentary news articles and share the hierarchical structure of goals to increase the transparency of social movements or projects,

Input through deliberative processes will occur after "seed data" are gathered in these three ways.

2   Linked Open Data of Public Issues and Goals

We designed LOD of public issues and goals in our previous research [5] and specialized them through developing the GoalShare [6] outlined in Figure 1. The classes `socia:Goal` and `socia:Issue` have titles and descriptions as textual content, and are linked with a related geographical region by `dcterms:spatial`,

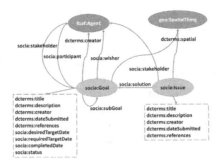

Fig. 1. Data model for describing public issues and goals

a creator by `dcterms:creator`, and created date by `dcterms:dateSubmitted`. The `socia:Goal` class especially has links to subgoals by `socia:subGoal` to represent the hierarchical structure and links to participants by `socia:participant` to represent a team of collaborators.

In our previous research, we constructed a dataset consisting of 657 public goals for recovery and revitalization from the Great East Japan Earthquake [5]. The goals were manually extracted from 96 news articles and two related documents on the Web.

After preliminary investigations using the dataset, the data model has been specialized for implementing GoalShare. The prototype of GoalShare has an RDF triple store and a SPARQL endpoint powered by OpenLink Virtuoso[1]. These 657 goals for earthquake recovery and new issues/goals created by Goal-Share users are stored in the RDF triple store. The user-generated goals are linked with personal identifiers with existing SNSs (Facebook and Twitter) and geographical identifiers with existing geographical LODs (GeoNames[2] and Ge-oLOD[3]). These links to the data hub potentially contribute to the interoperability of our dataset, which results from the LOD approach. The dataset needs to be interoperable to facilitate collaboration among existing groups on Facebook.

The goals and issues in our RDF triple store have openly been published via our SPARQL endpoint, `http://collab.open-opinion.org/sparql`. For example, the following SPARQL query returns the following RDF triples that represent a public goal for measures against earthquakes in Nagoya city.

```
SELECT * WHERE {
 GRAPH <http://collab.open-opinion.org> {
  <http://collab.open-opinion.org/resource/Goal/03095428-acbc-a9c9-0b91-9d386b8407f4> ?p ?o.
 }
}
```

```
<http://collab.open-opinion.org/resource/Goal/03095428-acbc-a9c9-0b91-9d386b8407f4>
 rdf:type socia:Goal;
 dcterms:title "Measures against the coming earthquake at Nankai Trough";
 dcterms:creator <http://collab.open-opinion.org/resource/Person/f5b8e09ac510>;
 dcterms:spatial <http://geolod.ex.nii.ac.jp/resource/EqBQEA>;
 dcterms:dateSubmitted "2013-12-09T14:00:00+09:00"^^xsd:dateTime;
 dcterms:references <http://www.nikkei.com/article/DGXNASFD3000F_Q3A530C1CN8000/>;
 socia:subGoal <http://collab.open-opinion.org/resource/Goal/a0d4b89fe3f3>;
 socia:subGoal <http://collab.open-opinion.org/resource/Goal/9d386b8407f4>;
 socia:desiredTargetDate "2015-01-01"^^xsd:date.
```

3   Development of GoalShare

3.1   Design of User Interface

There is a screenshot of the user interface of the current prototype of GoalShare [6] in Figure 2. It has a multilingual user interface (English, Japanese, and Finnish)

---

[1] `http://virtuoso.openlinksw.com/`

[2] `http://www.geonames.org/`

[3] `http://geolod.ex.nii.ac.jp/`

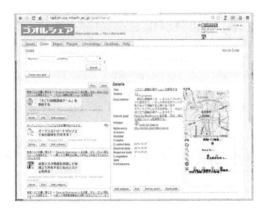

Fig. 2. User Interface of GoalShare

and is available via http://radish.ics.nitech.ac.jp/goalshare/. Although it currently supports logins with Facebook accounts, users also can input issues or goals anonymously without logins. Since we assumed that recent public goals would be suitable for understanding overviews of social movements or projects, the "Goals" tab is first opened in Figure 2 when users access the above URL. In the "Goals" tab, the most recently created goals are listed on the left of the figure. Details on the selected goal are on the right of the figure. The detailed section includes a map of related regions linked with the selected goal and a hierarchical visualization of subgoals and supergoals of the selected goal.

The detailed section contains buttons for "Add subgoal", "Edit", "Similar goals", and "Participates". Users can break down the selected goal into more concrete subgoals with the "Add subgoal" button and find goals similar to the selected goal with the "Similar goals" button. The method we used for calculating similarities is described in a later subsection. Moreover, users can register themselves as participants of the selected goal with the "Participants" button. We assumed that such functions effectively increased motivation for planning solutions and contributed to resolving issues.

Although sharing public goals on the "Goals" tab is essential to facilitate collaboration among motivated citizens, gathering issues on the "Issues" tab should occur prior to constructing goal structures because sharing issues can be the first cue to resolving public issues. Additionally, inputting issue data is easier for most citizens than creating hierarchical goal structures because public issues can be noticed in daily life. Inputting public goals as solutions requires thinking and planning through deliberative processes. Hence, the "Issues" tab provides an "Add as a goal" button to create an abstract goal as a solution to selected issues.

The validity of these prototype designs needs to be tested, verified, and improved through actual use by citizens to enable practical application in real-world societies.

3.2   Goal Generation from Twitter

We implemented a module for creating issues and goals in GoalShare from Twitter[4]. Twitter is a social media microblog service where users can post and read short text messages called Tweets. The length of a tweet is limited to 140 characters, and it can contain user defined topics known as hashtags that are marked with a "#" prefix. Tweets can be searched with hashtags, which allow individual Tweets to be grouped to conversations. One common way to use Twitter is in events, like conventions, so that there is a commonly known hashtag that participants append to tweets so that all tweets forms a conversation concerning that event.

In our research, Twitter presents multiple advantages. First, Twitter offers a HTTP API[5] for using the service programmatically. It enables us to search Tweets by topic, geographic location, and by tweeting users. Second, we can easily extract the textual content and while the text is written in natural language, Tweets have a clear convention for marking topics. In addition, Tweets can contain links to other internet materials that can be used as references in the generation of goal data. Moreover, users have to have accounts for posting Tweets, which we can use in GoalShare. The concepts of users are important in GoalShare. Users related goal information is used in the function for recommending potential collaborators for identifying similar types of users.

The implemented module searches periodically Tweets concerning predefined sets of hashtags. The first hashtag set is a collection of topics, like "#goalshare", that defines monitored conversations. We defined the second set as action keywords, like "#goal" and "#issue", which are used to determine the user's intention to create an item in questions in GoalShare. With this method, we can generate goals from specific conversations and label the generated GoalShare items accordingly.

When an unprocessed Tweet with these hashtags is encountered, the module extracts the following data from the Tweet: Tweet's unique identification code, text content, hashtags, and information about the tweeting user. First, the module creates a user for the system with Twitter information, like a name and an avatar image. The user is visually represented by the avatar in GoalShare. Second, the module uses the GoalShare HTTP API to generate an item, a goal or an issue, in GoalShare with the extracted Tweet data.

In future work on the Twitter export module, we plan to add automatic suggestion of issues without the user needing to use specific hashtags. Since a training corpus of social issues and goals is needed for this research plan, we intend to gather Tweets on issues and goals with the hashtags as positive examples in the corpus. Such a corpus can also openly be published as LOD to contribute to the research field of natural language processing.

---

[4] http://twitter.com
[5] https://dev.twitter.com/

4   Calculating Similarity between Goals

4.1   Methodology

In our previous research, we proposed a method of calculating the similarities between goals [5], which took into account surficial features in textual content, latent semantic features obtained with Latent Dirichlet Allocation (LDA) [9], and contextual features of linked subgoals. Additionally, we used an implementation of the hierarchical Dirichlet process-LDA (HDP-LDA)[6] in the training phase of a topic model [10].

However, we found that supergoals also contained contextual information by analyzing a dataset of 657 goals on recovery from the Great East Japan Earthquake. Moreover, the previous method overemphasized contextual features when there were few linked subgoals and supergoals. After this analysis, we improved the method of calculation [6]. The similarity between public goals g_i and g_j can be calculated using bag-of-features vectors $\mathrm{bof}(g_i)$ and $\mathrm{bof}(g_j)$.

$$\mathrm{sim}(g_i, g_j) = \frac{\mathrm{bof}(g_i) \cdot \mathrm{bof}(g_j)}{\|\mathrm{bof}(g_i)\|\|\mathrm{bof}(g_j)\|}, \tag{1}$$

$$\mathrm{bof}(g) = \frac{1 - \gamma(g)}{\|\mathrm{bof}_{\mathrm{self}}(g)\|}\mathrm{bof}_{\mathrm{self}}(g) + \frac{\gamma(g)}{\|\mathrm{bof}_{\mathrm{cntxt}}(g)\|}\mathrm{bof}_{\mathrm{cntxt}}(g), \tag{2}$$

$$\mathrm{bof}_{\mathrm{self}}(g) = \frac{\alpha}{\|\mathrm{tfidf}(g)\|}\mathrm{tfidf}(g) + \frac{\beta}{\|\mathrm{lda}(g)\|}\mathrm{lda}(g), \tag{3}$$

$$\mathrm{tfidf}(g) = \begin{pmatrix} \mathrm{tfidf}(w_1, g) \\ \vdots \\ \mathrm{tfidf}(w_{|W|}, g) \\ 0 \\ \vdots \\ 0 \end{pmatrix} \in \mathbb{R}^{|W|+|Z|}, \ \mathrm{lda}(g) = \begin{pmatrix} 0 \\ \vdots \\ 0 \\ \mathrm{p}(z_1|g) \\ \vdots \\ \mathrm{p}(z_{|Z|}|g) \end{pmatrix} \in \mathbb{R}^{|W|+|Z|}, \tag{4}$$

$$\mathrm{bof}_{\mathrm{cntxt}}(g) = \sum_{subg \in \mathrm{sub}(g)} \mathrm{bof}_{\mathrm{sub}}(subg) + \sum_{supg \in \mathrm{sup}(g)} \mathrm{bof}_{\mathrm{sup}}(supg), \tag{5}$$

$$\mathrm{bof}_{\mathrm{sub}}(g) = d_{\mathrm{sub}}\left(\mathrm{bof}_{\mathrm{self}}(g) + \sum_{subg \in \mathrm{sub}(g)} \mathrm{bof}_{\mathrm{sub}}(subg)\right), \tag{6}$$

$$\mathrm{bof}_{\mathrm{sup}}(g) = d_{\mathrm{sup}}\left(\mathrm{bof}_{\mathrm{self}}(g) + \sum_{supg \in \mathrm{sup}(g)} \mathrm{bof}_{\mathrm{sup}}(supg)\right), and \tag{7}$$

$$\gamma(g) = upper_{\mathrm{cntxt}} \cdot \tanh(k \cdot \|\mathrm{bof}_{\mathrm{cntxt}}(g)\|). \tag{8}$$

This is where g denotes a public goal, and $\mathrm{bof}(g)$ denotes a bag-of-features vector of g. Here, $\mathrm{sub}(g)$ denotes a set of subgoals of g, $\mathrm{sup}(g)$ denotes a set of supergoals of g, d_{sub} and d_{sup} denote decay ratios when recursively tracking subgoals and supergoals respectively. The $w \in W$ denotes a term, $z \in Z$ denotes

---

[6] http://www.cs.princeton.edu/~blei/topicmodeling.html

a latent topic derived by a latent topic model [9], and tfidf(w, g) denotes the TF-IDF, i.e., the product of term frequency and inverse document frequency, of w in a title and a description of g. Parameter $upper_{cntxt}$ denotes an upper limit of the weight of bof$_{cntxt}(g)$, $\alpha + \beta = 1$, and $0 \le \alpha$, β, $upper_{cntxt}$, d_{sub}, $d_{sup} \le 1$.

The two types of bag-of-feature vectors, bof$_{self}(g)$ and bof$_{cntxt}(g)$, are newly defined to incorporate contextual information not only from subgoals but also from supergoals. The bof$_{self}(g)$ represents a bag-of-features vector only extracted from target goal g and bof$_{cntxt}(g)$ represents a contextual bag-of-features vector extracted from subgoals and supergoals.

To recommend similar goals, a pair of goals g_i and g_j satisfying sim$(g_i, g_j) >$ θ_g is linked by the property schema:isSimilarTo that has been defined by schema.org[7]. Note that there are goal pairs that are not suitable to link by using schema:isSimilarTo despite large similarities, i.e., goal pairs that are already linked by the socia:subGoal property or goal pairs that have the same wishers or the same participants because such goal pairs already have collaborative relationships and do not need to be matched or recommended. Hence, such cases are filtered out when linking similar goals by using the schema:isSimilarTo property.

4.2   Experiments: Contextual Effects of Subgoals and Supergoals

The proposed method of calculating the similarities between goals requires parameters α, β, d_{sup}, d_{sub}, $upper_{cntxt}$, and k to be empirically set. Although quantitative optimization of the parameter set needs training data consisting of

Table 1. Similarity ranking of goal pairs where $\alpha = \beta = 0.5$, $d_{sup} = d_{sub} = 0.4$, $upper_{cntxt} = 0.5$, and $k = 0.7$

Rank	Similarity	Pair of goal titles (translated from Japanese)	
1	0.998	Selling ginkgoes	Selling "Fukushima Organic Cotton Babe"
2	0.901	Forming a new political party	Describing the process for forming a new political party
3	0.820	Completing projects for quake recovery	Securing quake recovery budgets
4	0.815	Promoting recognizable recovery in Miyako city	Conducting lessons on disaster prevention at elementary schools in Miyako city
5	0.797	Ensuring employment in Yamada-machi	Ensuring employment
6	0.778	Tree-planting ceremony in praying for quake recovery	Securing quake recovery budgets
7	0.776	Appropriate uses of quake recovery budgets	Securing quake recovery budgets
8	0.769	Sending public donations for quake recovery	Securing quake recovery budgets
9	0.768	Expanding targeted areas for support throughout Fukushima prefecture	Supporting victims who were evacuated outside of targeted area for support
10	0.766	Decontamination of radiation	Certifying decontamination contractors

---

[7] http://schema.org/Product

positive examples (pairs of similar goals suitable for matching or recommendations) and negative examples (goals pairs unsuitable for matching or recommendations), it is not easy to construct such training data because clear definitions of suitability for matching or recommendations are not obvious and are difficult.

As preliminary experiments, we respectively varied d_{sup} and d_{sub} to qualitatively investigate the effects of taking into account supergoals and subgoals. A subset of 100 goals chosen from the LOD of goals for earthquake recovery were used in the experiments. The parameter set as the basis for reference before varying them was $\alpha = \beta = 0.5$, $d_{sup} = d_{sub} = 0.4$, $upper_{cntxt} = 0.5$, and $k = 0.7$. In this parameter setting, the decay ratios for supergoals and subgoals, d_{sup} and d_{sub}, took the same value of 0.4. The top ten similarity rankings of goal pairs for the reference parameter setting are listed in Table 1. These ten pairs were not greatly affected by the contextual features and decay ratios d_{sup} and d_{sub} because they shared the same vocabularies. The $bof_{self}(g)$ consisting of surficial and semantic features should be close in each pair. Thus, the top ten pairs were not drastically changed when varying d_{sup} and d_{sub}. To qualitatively investigate the effects of supergoals and subgoals as textual features, we observed goal pairs whose ranks were drastically raised by increasing the decay ratios. Tables 2 and 3

Table 2. Goal pairs whose rank is raised by emphasizing supergoals, i.e., increasing d_{sup} from 0.4 to 0.8

Rank gain	Rank	Similarity	Pair of goal titles (translated from Japanese)	
54	16	0.738	Saving victims' unborn children	Supporting victims who were evacuated outside targeted area for support
36	68	0.645	Limiting use of quake recovery budgets to recovery and relief for victims	Supporting victims who were evacuated outside of targeted area for support
24	28	0.723	Enhancing concretized policies based on Victims' Protection Law	Committee for concretizing Victims' Protection Law organizes public forum for victims across nation
22	59	0.659	Setting up contact lines for Victims Protection Law	Supporting victims who were evacuated outside of targeted area for support
18	17	0.737	Citizen participation to decontaminate radiation	Speeding up decontamination of radiation

Table 3. Goal pairs whose rank is raised by emphasizing subgoals, i.e., increasing d_{sub} from 0.4 to 0.8

Rank gain	Rank	Similarity	Pair of goal titles (translated from Japanese)	
69	49	0.691	Supplying aid for relief of victims	Organizing events for friendship exchanges between evacuated victims and local residents
67	40	0.709	Recovery in Iwate prefecture	Tree-planting ceremony in praying for quake recovery
56	32	0.721	Recovery in Iwate prefecture	Completing projects for quake recovery
56	59	0.683	Recovery in Iwate prefecture	Promoting recognizable recovery in Miyako city
53	31	0.724	Recovery in Iwate prefecture	Securing quake recovery budgets

respectively show goal pairs whose ranks are greatly raised when d_{sup} becomes 0.8 and d_{sub} becomes 0.8. "Rank gain" represents how the rank was raised by increasing the decay ratio and "Rank" represents the raised rank. Whereas Table 2 shows that increasing d_{sup} affected relatively concrete goals and the highly affected ranks could be raised to higher than the 20th rank, Table 3 shows that increasing d_{sub} affected abstract goals such as "Recovery in Iwate prefecture" and "Supplying aid for relief of victims" and the highly affected ranks could not be raised to higher than the 30th rank. These results indicate that emphasizing contextual features in supergoals is more appropriate than emphasizing them in subgoals because concrete goals are more suitable for recommendations than abstract ones.

5   Trial Workshop for Citizens

To improve the system design of GoalShare through actual use, a trial workshop was held on Dec. 19, 2013 in Ogaki city in Gifu prefecture in Japan. The trial workshop was organized as part of a series of events called "Open data cafe" managed by CCL Inc[8]. Twelve citizens participated in the workshop. There is an illustration provided to participants, which explains the structure of an issue and its solution as hierarchical goals, in Figure 3(a). Participants were divided into three groups. They first wrote regional issues on sticky notes and selected one issue though debate. They then hierarchically structured the goals to solve the selected issue and then input the issue and goal hierarchy into the GoalShare prototype.

After the trial use, participants responded to the three statements in a questionnaire about the service concept of GoalShare.

S1. After GoalShare is officially launched, I want to use this service.

S2. After public issues and goals are accumulated in GoalShare, social movements will be easier to understand.

S3. After public issues and goals are accumulated in GoalShare, participating in or contributing to solving regional issues will be easier, even for people unfamiliar with regional contexts.

The results from the questionnaire are shown in Figure 4, which indicates that two-thirds of participants agreed with S1 and S2 and over 80% of participants agreed with S3. Moreover, participants returned positive feedback suggestions to improve the design of the prototype. For example, they suggested incorporating group accounts to find civic groups and attaching tags to issues/goals to represent concerns or topics. We are planning to continuously organize such events to improve the participatory design process of GoalShare.

---

[8] http://opendatacafe.blogspot.jp/2013/12/inlod_20.html (in Japanese)

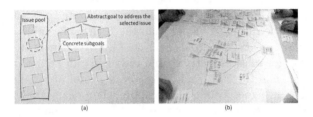

Fig. 3. (a) Illustration for workshop participants and (b) actual issues/goals written by participants

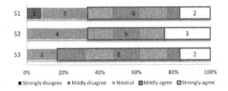

Fig. 4. Results from questionnaire after workshop in Ogaki city

6   Related Work and our Research Context

6.1   Project Management

Goals in the research field of project management are commonly structured as hierarchies by subdividing goals into subgoals. Instances of such structures are seen in the Thinking Process of the Theory of Constraint (TOC) [11] and the Work Breakdown Structure (WBS) in the Project Management Body of Knowledge (PMBOK) [12]. Although these models are generally used for project management within an organization, some researchers have applied them to public sector problems. TOC, especially, has been tried to be applied to recovery from disasters [13,14]. Logic Models are also commonly used in the public sector for managing participatory program planning [15]. Logic Models are also used to deal with public issues and goals because building a logic model first requires issue statements and goal statements [16].

There are many Web applications for sharing tasks and managing projects, e.g., Trello[9], Cyboze Live[10], and Backlog[11]. Flying Logic[12] is a software for struc-

---

[9] http://trello.com/
[10] http://cybozulive.com/
[11] http://www.backlog.jp/
[12] http://flyinglogic.com/

turing goal hierarchies based on TOC. However, they do not support functions for sharing goals on finding potential collaborators in public spheres. The originality of our study is dealing with goal hierarchies as open data and utilizing them to facilitate public collaboration.

6.2   Civic Tech

Open data technology has recently had a great affinity for the civic tech sector, i.e., technical communities for creating participatory improvements to governmental services using information technology. The development process for new tools through public collaboration such as "hackathon" events can be shared as public goals and related issues. Civic tech sector has been activated in Japan since 2013. Within this social context, the Code for Japan[13] was organized by reference to the Code for America[14] in 2013, and many hackathon events also have been organized. Continuous developments after the event were not very frequent in the hackathon in Japan, because development team members were not so many and were often holiday volunteers. We are planning to apply Goal-Share to such problems, i.e., we have assumed that sharing issues and goals dealt with by civic tech communities would enable the development projects to find potential collaborators and to continue to solve the issues solving through software development. We developed a goal generation function using Twitter to be used in such civic tech events. The function can use hashtags specified by hackathon events because such events often announce their specific hashtags to participants.

6.3   Structured Argumentation

Structuring and visualizing argumentation effectively support eParticipation [17]. There are currently several tools for structuring and visualizing argumation, i.e., Evidence Hub [18], MIT Deliberatorium [19], etc. These tools typically produce "box and arrow" diagrams in which premises and conclusions are formulated as statements [20]. The hierarchical structures of public goals created by GoalShare users can be regarded as types of such diagrams. Moreover, the hierarchy of public goals can be a hub of argumentation networks because deliberative argumentation is needed for negotiation processes between potential collaborators by them comparing their goal hierarchies. Such argumentation data need to be linked with a shared goal hierarchy to ensure openness when they collaboratively conduct their shared plan. Developing a function for deliberation in the negotiation process based on goal hierarchies is an important future work.

7   Conclusion

We developed GoalShare, which is a prototype goal matching service in the public sphere. It was implemented as a Web application to match citizens who

---

[13] http://code4japan.org/
[14] http://codeforamerica.org/

had similar public goals. Our system was based on an LODset of public issues and goal hierarchies, which was openly published via a SPARQL end point. The interoperability of dataset, due to the LOD approach, is required to facilitate collaboration among existing groups in existing SNSs. We formulated a similarity metric between public goals on the basis of bag-of-features vectors consisting of surficial features, latent semantic features, and contextual features. To determine the optimal parameters in our formulation, empirical investigations using an actual dataset were needed. We conducted experiments to quantitatively investigate what effects the contextual features of supergoals and subgoals had by using actual public goals about disaster recovery in Japan. The results indicate that the contextual features in supergoals should be emphasized more than those in subgoals. Moreover, we held a trial workshop for citizens and obtained positive feedback from participants.

We are planning to develop a function to support deliberative argumentation for negotiation processes between potential collaborators by comparing their goal hierarchies and a function to match citizens who have complementary skill set or resources in future work. Improvements to GoalShare will be conducted with the help of user feedbacks in trial workshops or hackathon events.

Acknowledgments. We greatly appreciate support by the Ogaki office of CCL Inc. for organizing the trial workshop of GoalShare. This work was supported by a Grant-in-Aid for Young Scientists (B) (No. 25870321) from JSPS.

References

1. Motesharrei, S., Rivas, J., Kalnay, E.: Human and Nature Dynamics (HANDY): Modeling inequality and use of resources in the collapse or sustainability of societies. Ecological Economics 101, 90–102 (2014)
2. Shi, P., Li, N., Ye, Q., Dong, W., Han, G., Fang, W.: Research on integrated disaster risk governance in the context of global environmental change. International Journal of Disaster Risk Science 1(1), 17–23 (2010)
3. Yamamoto, K.: Volunteer activities in time of disaster in japan's highly information-oriented society. Journal of Earth Science and Engineering 3(3), 190–202 (2013)
4. Yamaguchi, M., Maguth, B.: Using social networking in the social studies for global citizenship: A case study of japan's 3:11 quake. In: Proceedings of Society for Information Technology & Teacher Education International Conference 2012, pp. 3260–3287 (2012)
5. Shiramatsu, S., Ozono, T., Shintani, T.: Approaches to assessing public concerns: Building linked data for public goals and criteria extracted from textual content. In: Wimmer, M.A., Tambouris, E., Macintosh, A. (eds.) ePart 2013. LNCS, vol. 8075, pp. 109–121. Springer, Heidelberg (2013)
6. Tossavainen, T., Shiramatsu, S., Ozono, T., Shintani, T.: Implementing a system enabling open innovation by sharing public goals based on linked open data. In: Ali, M., Pan, J.-S., Chen, S.-M., Horng, M.-F. (eds.) IEA/AIE 2014, Part II. LNCS, vol. 8482, pp. 98–108. Springer, Heidelberg (2014)

7. Roth, A.E., Sotomayor, M.A.O.: Two-Sided Matching: A Study in Game-Theoretic Modeling and Analysis. Econometric Society Monographs, vol. 18. Cambridge University Press, Cambridge (1990)
8. Kim, S., Mabin, V.J., Davies, J.: The theory of constraints thinking processes: retrospect and prospect. International Journal of Operations & Production Management 28(2), 155–184 (2008)
9. Blei, D.M., Ng, A.Y., Jordan, M.I.: Latent Dirichlet Allocation. Journal of Machine Learning Research 3, 993–1022 (2003)
10. Teh, Y., Jordan, M., Beal, M., Blei, D.: Hierarchical dirichlet processes. Journal of the American Statistical Association 101(476), 1566–1581 (2006)
11. AGI: The theory of constraints and its thinking processes - a brief introduction to toc, http://www.goldratt.com/pdfs/toctpwp.pdf (2009)
12. PMI: A Guide to the Project Management Body of Knowledge, 4th edn. Project Management Institute (2008)
13. Cheng, J., Shigekawa, K., Meguro, K., Yamazaki, F., Nakagawa, I., Hayashi, H., Tamura, K.: Applying the toc logistic process to clarify the problem schemes of near-field earthquake in tokyo metropolitan area. Journal of social safety science (11), 225–233 (2009) (in Japanese)
14. Ohara, M., Kondo, S., Kou, T., Numada, M., Meguro, K.: Overview of social issues after the great east-japan earthquake disaster - part 3 of activity reports of 3.11net tokyo. SEISAN KENKYU 63(6), 749–754 (2011) (in Japanese)
15. McLaughlin, J.A., Jordan, G.B.: Logic models: a tool for telling your programs performance story. Evaluation and program planning 22(1), 65–72 (1999)
16. Innovation Network: Logic model workbook, http://www.innonet.org/client_docs/File/logic_model_workbook.pdf (2005)
17. Benn, N., Macintosh, A.: Argument visualization for eparticipation: towards a research agenda and prototype tool. In: Tambouris, E., Macintosh, A., de Bruijn, H. (eds.) ePart 2011. LNCS, vol. 6847, pp. 60–73. Springer, Heidelberg (2011)
18. De Liddo, A., Buckingham Shum, S.: The Evidence Hub: Harnessing the collective intelligence of communities to build evidence-based knowledge. In: 6th International Conference on Communities and Technologies, Large-Scale Idea Management and Deliberation Systems Workshop (2013)
19. Iandoli, L., Klein, M., Zolla, G.: Enabling online deliberation and collective decision making through large-scale argumentation: A new approach to the design of an internet-based mass collaboration platform. International Journal of Decision Support System Technology 1(1), 69–92 (2009)
20. van den Braak, S.W., van Oostendorp, H., Prakken, H., Vreeswijk, G.A.W.: A critical review of argument visualization tools: Do users become better reasoners? In: Workshop Notes of the ECAI-2006 Workshop on CMNA, pp. 67–75 (2006)

Evaluation of an E-participation Project: Lessons Learned and Success Factors from a Cross-Cultural Perspective

Peter Parycek, Michael Sachs, Florian Sedy, and Judith Schossböck

Danube University Krems, Dr. Karl Dorrek-Straße 30, A-3500 Krems, Austria
{peter.parycek,michael.sachs,florian.sedy,
judith.schossboeck}@donau-uni.ac.at

Abstract. In the area of large-scale e-participation projects on a cross-national level, the project we present is based on the idea that the active involvement of young people in the process of socio-political decision-making plays an important societal role. OurSpace is a multi-national project supporting a closer relationship between European decision makers, and Europe's younger generation. OurSpace tried to combine ICT usage, young peoples' readiness and motivation to participate, and their assumed lack of information regarding European politics. We present the evaluation framework and methodology applied for OurSpace, the major results of the project evaluation, and the lessons learned from a comparative perspective.

Keywords: e-participation, online deliberation, evaluation, youth, Europe.

1 Introduction

Citizenship builds upon our right to participation, and ideally participation should be equal, inclusive and made as easy as possible. Due to the increased usage of the internet and the democratic deficit felt, e-participation projects are often based on the idea to facilitate participation and to attract the attention of a specific target group, in particular those attracted to the usage of ICT. E-participation experts have emphasised that further investigation should be done in two areas: first, the „applicability of e-participation tools to particular contexts", and second „assessing the social acceptance of e-participation", i.e. the evaluation of such projects and tools [1]. Conceptualising the methodological frameworks of e-participation evaluation has thus become a relevant topic in the field [2]. OurSpace is a multi-national project specifically aimed towards bringing European politics and decision makers closer to the European youth. Young people are principally motivated to participate [9] in participating in political online forms and they often prefer online to offline forms [10]. They are frequently seen to possess the necessary capabilities for e-participation projects due to having grown up with digital media. The term „Digital Natives"[2] (often falsely) implies that those who grew up with the internet also navigate more

E. Tambouris et al. (Eds.): ePart 2014, LNCS 8654, pp. 128–140, 2014.

easily in online environments. Obviously, to use ICTs for participation also requires cognitive capabilities that enable the individual to decide between alternative opportunities and to recognise them in an online environment.

The methodology covered technical suitability and usability as well as young people's opinion on a specific deliberation tool. The following aspects were relevant:

- How do young people navigate in a multi-level e-participation environment?
- How relevant do they find the discussions and how much do they trust the outcome of this specific tool?
- Can e-participation projects for the young lead to more interest in politics or politicians from the target group?
- What can be said about the nature of discussions between the young and politicians online and how they interact?
- What chances and difficulties can be observed from a cross-national perspective, i.e. in cross-country online deliberation?

The EU project provided an online deliberation space designed to actively engage young European citizens, in particular young citizens from Austria, the Czech Republic, Greece and the United Kingdom.[1] These countries with different socio-economic situations ran pilots that promoted the project on both the national and European level. The project provides an online deliberation space designed to actively engage young European citizens.

2   Evaluation Methodology

Building on already existing research on e-participation evaluation, the OurSpace evaluation model offers a methodology with reference to the methodological framework developed by Macintosh [1] and extended by the consortium. In the following, the authors will describe the methodology, the tools and the circumstances of the evaluation. The evaluation of the open stage focused on a mix of qualitative and quantitative data. This data is related to the complete project, and interviews were done in the later project stages (since October 2013).[2] The external test stage, in autumn 2012, focused on 200 user tests, which covered important aspects of usability and functionality of the platform. The open stage started at the beginning of September 2012, when the platform was opened to users and promotional activities with the ambitious goal of engaging 6.000 users. By the end of March 2014, around 4.870 users have been registering on the platform.

The state of e-participation has been studied by the Demo-Net Network of Excellence: The country reports in Coleman et al. [4] emphasise context information

---

[1] See aims and scope oft he project under the official EU project site
http://www.ep-ourspace.eu/Project/Approach.aspx (accessed March 27th, 2014).

[2] For downloads of the Deliberables and Publications, see
http://ep-ourspace.eu/Downloads/Deliverables.aspx (accessed March 27th, 2014).

on institutional and political conditions. Several e-participation researchers highlight the importance of systematic analysis of processes and outcomes against predefined criteria [5]. They make the assumption that "benefits to be gained from evaluation are manifold" [5] e.g., identifying conditions and extent of success as well as deficits. In the context of OurSpace, evaluation models provide a structured analysis model for estimating how far an e-participation project can help to enhance certain aspects of democracy like citizens interest in politics. The evaluation of e-participation is still in its infancy and there is a need to develop a coherent framework, encompassing a range of perspectives and research methods [6]. The OurSpace project seeks to adopt the assumption that contexts frame some participation processes and will take a closer look at the political and social perspective of evaluation, which is reflected in the relevant indicator categories of the evaluation methodology.

2.1   Tools

Online Questionnaires: For the final evaluation, two different questionnaires were conducted: A short questionnaire for direct integration into the website, which users reached via a feedback button directly on the website and a long questionnaire with detailed questions. 310 feedback questionnaires were filled in and 76 were counted, whereas for the long questionnaire, the evaluation builds on 420 responses.

Interviews (3 experts, 12 users, 6 decision makers): Three types of interviews were conducted: Users, experts and decision makers in all pilot countries. Whereas the guidelines were constructed for face-to-face interviews, only user and expert interviews were done in person. Most of the decision maker interviews were done in written form due to time constraints of this target group. The interviews were conducted in November and December 2013. Interview guidelines followed the relevant indicator levels of the evaluation methodology. The user category refers to citizens that have chosen to register for OurSpace services and have been active on the site. Decision makers interviewed included representatives from political parties, officials from the EU, and national or regional agencies. The interviews with experts were done with national and international e-participation experts.

Discourse Analysis: Aspects of online deliberation from a qualitative perspective were analysed according to pre-defined criteria: Pilots analysed exemplary discussions on the platform according to criteria for successful online deliberation. For this analysis, all pilots chose two topics relevant for discourse analysis, most of them being successful discussions with significant numbers of user comments.

Evaluation Workshop (12/2013): Additionally to the tools described above, the consortium conducted a focus group dedicated to the evaluation. This workshop took one and a half days and was organised by DUK, and took place in London on December 5-6, when most data had been collected and pre-assessed. In the focus group the main outcomes, conclusions, and recommendations of the OurSpace project were discussed.

Platform Data and Google Analytics: By using the available platform data in combination with Google Analytics it was possible to evaluate activities during the project period. Furthermore, data from social media platforms like Facebook and statistics related to the OurSpace blogs were analysed.

2.2   Overview of the OurSpace Methodology

Studies focusing on e-participation effects and evaluation have increased over the last few years [7]. In this context, several conceptual and methodological frameworks have been proposed. Kubicek et al. [8] introduce a structural model for analysing and evaluating participation initiatives on a general level. The Demo-Net consortium – elaborating on Macintosh and Whyte [1] – suggests a three-layered model stressing different levels of e-participation objectives, an approach that integrates the following perspectives: Project perspective, socio-technical perspective and democratic perspective. The OurSpace methodology adapted this approach suggested in Macintosh and Whyte [1]. Kubicek et al. [8] also analysed participation projects with relation to their success and defined success factors in relation to the existence of "strong links to formal political decision making" [8]. This perspective was covered with various questions in the OurSpace evaluation: Both users' opinion on the outcomes of the projects as well as decision makers opinion regarding the actual impact of the discussions were analysed. The category of the political as context factor has been added to the OurSpace evaluation framework, whilst putting less emphasis on the project perspective.

OurSpace as a multilingual project with a multi-national, European focus has to take into account several political, but also socio-cultural frameworks. In this paper, results of the different evaluation perspectives will be summarised and should be interpreted and read along the different political situations. The methodological overview is influenced by the framework of Aichholzer and Westholm [5], who link different aspects along the three layer evaluation model to the relevant methodology. The OurSpace evaluation builds on two main perspectives of the project; a technological and a socio-political perspective. The categories as proposed by Macintosh have been further divided into four *evaluation level categories*.

1. A *political* evaluation level: Although the democracy perspective and political aspects are the most difficult ones to analyse, OurSpace, according to one of the main goals of the project, respectively evoking young people's interest for politics and democracy, focused on aspects of influence on political decision-making and relevance of the discussed topic for politicians and decision makers involved in this level.
2. A *technical* evaluation level: On this level, platform and tools usability and suitability were assessed.
3. A *social* evaluation level: The social perspective covers aspects of society related to community-orientation and connection more than aspects of politics and decision making. On the social level, community-building and (digital) connections between users will be measured. Special emphasis is also given on the integration of multiple communication channels (web, mobile and social media channels).

4. A *methodological evaluation level*: This level comprises *methodological questions* related to the effectiveness of the essential success factors and characteristics of the platform: The deliberation model, dissemination activities and the effectiveness of user engagement tactics.

Translating these perspectives into indicator categories, the OurSpace evaluation framework comprises the following categories:

- *Political level*: 1. Relevancy and Popularity of selected deliberation themes, 2. Effectiveness of communicating the trial results to decision makers and relevant public bodies, 3. Degree of influence on decision-making processes and political actions
- *Technical level*: 1. Platforms and tools usability, 2. Platform purpose suitability
- *Social level*: 1. Effectiveness of integrating multiple evaluation tools, 2. Digital connections created between users, 3. Quality of discussion and deliberation process
- *Methodological level*: 1. Effectiveness of deliberation model, 2. Effectiveness of dissemination activities, 3. Effectiveness of user engagement tactics.

3   Results

The following refers to the most visible results with reference to all pilot countries. In accordance with other findings of user activity in e-participation, there was only a small amount of users actively posting on the website in relation to those just "lurking" and not getting active. Most other users used participation options with a lower participation threshold, such as likes and thumbing, which is sometimes also known as gamification elements in e-participation [11]. Since launch of the platform, the site has counted 52.000+ visitors, 29.000+ unique visitors, 338.000+ page visits and 18+ active decision-makers. The average user looked at 6+ pages and stays for 6+ minutes. On the technical level, users were satisfied with the technical features and functionality of the platform. Around 60 % liked the look and feel of the platform, and 74 % in total found it easy to navigate. Despite those good results, observations of workshop leaders also revealed that there were sometimes difficulties with navigation, and additional guidance, in particular regarding the stages of the evaluation process and regarding the possibility to post proposals, were needed. Suggestions for improvement on the basis of interviews and the questionnaires included wishes for a more modern design, the enhancing of visibility and more interconnectivity. Users wanted to create groups between members and add more information about users.

3.1   Political Level: Interest in Politics and Trust

Regarding the relevance and popularity of the selected topics, experts, users and decision makers were generally very positive about the topics (74 % of youth stated they found the topics relevant or very relevant). Users were able to create their own topics on the platform (which might have influenced this result to the positive).

Table 1. Relevance of deliberation themes for youth

PC1.5.3 Short questionnaire: How relevant do you consider the content on the OurSpace platform?					
	Very relevant	Relevant	Neither relevant nor irrelevant	Not very relevant	Not at all relevant	Responses
ALL	33,33 %	57,33 %	8,00 %	0 %	1,33 %	75

One of the major challenges of the project was to get young people in contact with decision makers who participated not equally throughout the countries, and continuous contact with decision makers was needed. Those who participated engaged actively with youth and most of the time also addressed them directly. The discourse analysis showed that in most cases decision makers only gave feedback one time and youth did not respond a second time to that feedback. Despite a few successful showcases of engaging decision makers, users still asked for more decision maker involvement, and in some countries they were almost completely absent. In Austria and due to direct contact with politicians decision makers responded to almost every thread they opened, and 40 % of MEPs participated on the platform by opening their own topic. In Greece, no decision maker participated actively in discussions. In the UK, two MEPs answered in the results phase, but not during the discussions.

Users and decision makers agreed on the potential of the platform but were indifferent about the impact on political work. Those politicians who participated in the platform were very positive about the impact on their political work, albeit this can be seen as mostly inspirational impact. In the Czech Republic, actual policies were discussed and users were therefore slightly more positive about the platform impact on such policies. Users were indifferent regarding whether the platform made them more interested in the work of a politician. Results of the questionnaire showed that they were positive regarding the potential of an e-participation tool to bridge the gap between decision makers and youth, and 75 % stated in the questionnaire that they think platforms like OurSpace are good to get involved or more interested in politics.

Table 2. Potential of e-participation platform for getting more interested in politics

Long questionnaire: Taking into consideration the above, do you think that platforms like OurSpace are good to get involved or more interested in politics?					
	Yes	Rather yes	Neutral	Rather no	No	Responses
AT	46,15 %	26,63 %	13,61 %	6,51 %	7,10 %	169
CZ	29,53 %	30,23 %	2,33 %	9,30 %	18,60 %	43
GR	25 %	42 %	25 %	5 %	4 %	85
UK	42 %	47 %	6 %	2 %	3 %	64
ALL	40,06 %	34,73 %	12,61 %	5,60 %	7,00 %	357

Users were indifferent (and slightly more positive in CZ) regarding the question whether they would be more interested in the work of a politician in the interviews.

Table 3. E-participation platform and getting more interested in the life of a politician

Questionnaire: Did you get more interested in the work of a politician that you met/that posted on OurSpace?						
	Yes	Rather yes	Neutral	Rather no	No	Responses
AT	17,96 %	25,15 %	29,94 %	10,18 %	16,77 %	167
CZ	16,28 %	27,91 %	16,28 %	18,60 %	20,93 %	43
GR	6 %	14 %	42 %	15 %	22 %	85
UK	21 %	19 %	37 %	6 %	16 %	62
ALL	15,41 %	21,85 %	32,49 %	11,76 %	18,49 %	357

Only 33 % stated the platform could improve their trust in politics, although they said the platform would have the potential to better informing users about political issues and making people more interested in politics. While most users did not find that the platform could improve trust in politics and politicians, a lot of them were also indifferent regarding that question (35 %). Czech users were far more positive in this regard: 81 % of Czech users found that the platform has helped them to improve their trust in politics and politicians, compared to 43 % of Austrian users. The worst result regarding trust and politics was seen in Greece: Only 18 % of Greek users stated it could help them to improve their trust in that matter. The importance of trust in politics has long been emphasised by political theorists, and there is evidence that this is still the case, in particular on national level [12]. The different numbers regarding trust in politics correspond with other comparative or national findings regarding trust. For instance, Austria is behind many CEE countries regarding trust in politics, and numbers have been going down considerable during recent years [13]. However, around 50 % of Austrians trust the Austrian government according to a 2014 survey by Gallup [14], and results of the OurSpace survey among young showed a similar picture like surveys among the general population in most pilot countries. Statistics also have shown that trust in politicians is higher on the local level [15], and e-participation projects have been related to the hope of bringing politicians closer to people by bringing them into direct contact with participants. The majority of young users felt empowered or very empowered (59 %) by the platform, based on the results of the short questionnaire that was put online. A bias has to be taken into account here as these responses were small in number and most likely coming from people who were very interested in the platform anyways, probably displaying a generally very positive view on e-participation. Summarizing, results show that the young are ready to engage and credit e-participation platforms much potential, but it is hard to engage people beyond the easy user group of already politically interested people.

3.2   Social Level: Inclusivity, Connections and Discussions

Emploeying social media channels was important for getting people engaged in the project and an essential part of the dissemination strategy. Mobile access, however, proved to be less important than expected: the majority of users accessed the site through regular means, i.e. the website version of the platform. It has to be pointed out that this is also due to engagement tactics and promotion strategies which clearly focused on the website version, whereas mobile versions like the Android application were only advertised throughout the beginning of the project and less so from the open stage, as they were not taken on by users. This shows that mobile applications will not be used automatically but have to be continuously promoted. Compared to the general access via the OurSpace platform (mobile and non-mobile), it has to be concluded that alternative forms of access like applications were less interesting for the typical OurSpace user than initially expected. This also correlates with data from Google Analytics: about 12 % used mobile devices to access the platform (however they did not use the Android app for this). Regarding registration, social media (Facebook Connect) was an important feature and 36 % of users registered via this option on the platform. Nonetheless, registration via email or Facebook Connect also opens up a barrier to participation, and it should be discussed whether registration is necessary at all stages of the deliberation process in e-participation in order to increase inclusivity. Links between users and decision makers have been made, yet participating decision makers faced time limits, which could be seen as a major obstacle to the sustainability of connections made and to getting feedback to the threads on the platform. However some countries were very successful regarding collecting decision maker feedback, e.g. Austria where every decision maker posted feedback to the thread they opened, although this had to be supported by continuous reminders and by contacting the offices of the politicians. The discourse analysis showed that discussions displayed a variety of users, gender and countries and in 6 cases, cross-national debates with users from three different countries were found. The tone of the discussion was generally friendly and content-related moderation almost not necessary. However, language could still be seen as major hurdle regarding cross-country deliberation, with most of the cross-national debates happening on the EU layer and in English. If moderation was required, it was mostly in relation to process, e.g. proposals that had been supported by moderators or comments turned into proposals, as only from 4 proposals a thread could reach the last phase of the deliberation process. Very often, despite users being very satisfied with the 4 stages of the model in the questionnaire and interviews (69 % were very satisfied or satisfied with the platform for political debate as a whole in the questionnaire), it seemed that they did not understand or realise those option, so it was often overseen by users. This had to be amended by moderators pointing out that option and sometimes turning comments including a solution into a proposal.

4   Lessons Learnt and Best Practices

The following section summarises the lessons learnt throughout the project related to quality of discussions as well as some parameters of analysis like transparency and the multi-level conception of the e-participation tool.

4.1   Best Practices Discussions (Deliberation Process)

The platform displayed different levels of activity in different pilot countries: Regarding the thumbs per pilot, it is visible that this activity is used in Austria more often than in the UK, related to the number of registered users. Users in the Czech Republic use this feature the most and more often than postings – this makes the Czech user a very active user compared to the average user in other countries. This underlines again that the Czech discussions are most vibrant and engaging, despite their position in the general user ranking. Of course, thumbs are no indicators of a good quality discussion but they indicate interest of the users in the discussion.

There has been active participation of decision makers (CZ, AT, UK) and the Austrian pilot can be seen as a best practices example of how to integrate decision makers in the discussion process. Crucial in this case was that moderation and community management was necessary, as well as constant reminders of decision makers or their offices to receive feedback or postings on the platform. This lead to the result that one third of all Austrian MEPs were active on the platform.

Controversial topics proved to be most successful and the topics mentioned in the pilots at a glance section give an overview about which topics have been most successful. Apart from that, topics that concerned the rights of a minority (e.g. rights of homosexuals), education (e.g. votes at 16) and environment (e.g. climate change) could be identified as topics with high potential for discussion. Moderation of topics was still necessary, both online (in particular reminders of MEPs and regarding the treatment of proposals (process-orientated moderation) and offline (e.g. guidance at workshops with youth regarding the platform or deliberation process).

4.2   Inclusiveness and Transparency

Regarding transparent and inclusive participation, OurSpace moderators followed a procedure to inform users about the reasons for deleting postings and so moderators were transparent in their moderation activities. All parties of the political spectrum and a broad variety of gender and age were invited, and user diversity showed that this was successful.

Regarding cross-country deliberation, the OurSpace platform offered the opportunity to engage in such discussions by using the Google Translate tool and keeping debates open for all users from every pilot country. However, language can still be seen as the major obstacle in cross-country deliberation.

Another barrier was people being increasingly critical about the registration process and giving away their e-mail (this is related to privacy concerns, but also related to avoiding spam or information overflow). This suggests that future models of registration should keep that barrier low. It is debatable whether all stages of the deliberation process or all e-participation stages in general ask for registration. Some users can be very critical about the registration process and both Facebook Connect and email registration offer major hurdles that have been confirmed by users in workshops and other feedback. However, as the platform was based on counting user numbers as well as further engagement increase by user recommendations, it was necessary to distinguish between registered and non-registered users in the OurSpace case.

4.3   Acceptance of the Four Stages Deliberation Model

There was general a good evaluation of the four stages evaluation model. E-participation expert Kühnberger mentioned in the interview that e-participation usually follows a layer approach, and different levels in e-participation are a common procedure. Users stated that the model helped them to be more politically informed and thus trusted that the platform enabled them to place better political decisions, as well as generally being more empowered in the area of politics. They credited the platform a lot of potential and were satisfied with the suitability of the platform for its purpose. However, even though users liked the deliberation model per se, the details of the four stages of the deliberation model, in particular the options to hand in proposals, wasn't understood or taken on by many users. Users also pointed out that they liked the cross-country approach of the deliberation model.

Summarising, users were satisfied with the technical features of the platform, in particular regarding the purpose of the platform. If there were suggestions for improvement, they were mostly related to interconnectivity and visibility, or requests for a guidance through the process, which the project reacted and responded accordingly by making certain threads more visible and by integrating an explanatory tool (page guideline) related to the four stages of the decision making process on the platform. It has to be noted that without moderation from the consortium and the community managers, the four stages of the model according to the previously defined rules (e.g. a significant number of proposals were necessary before a topic could reach the last phase) could not have been realised.

4.4   Barriers in Cross-Country Deliberation

The challenges in cross-country e-participation projects are still related to the feedback of decision makers, and despite good results in some countries (e.g. Austria) other countries like Greece decision makers almost didn't participate at all. The impact on policy making as perceived by users did not exceed the inspirational. Users were critical whether such projects would improve the general trust in politics and whether the socio-political conditions in the pilot countries seemed to be dominating the outcome of the project. Users did not trust the political impact of a debate, which can also be related to the general political climate in the European Union and in particular the pilot countries that played a role in the project. The different results on whether such projects could improve trust in politics confirm the importance of the different political and economic situation in the countries. Different forms of user activity in the pilot countries could also be related to this, e.g. less active users in the Greek pilot as compared to the Czech pilot, even though the Greek pilot brought a lot of users in terms of user registration.

As emphasised, understanding the different stages of the deliberation process proved to be difficult, and the possibility of handing in proposals needed moderation and support as did the last phase (voting phase) of the deliberation process. This shows that multi-layer processes in e-participation need a lot of explanation and moderation, even for young users, who are often seen to be equipped with the necessary capabilities to participate online more naturally.

Another challenge was related to the understanding of politically complex content: Concrete legislation is difficult to discuss for users for this requires profound knowledge and adequate time to place an argument properly. Additionally, it was difficult to engage a target group beyond politically already active users, and to get people participating in discussions outside their own country or language group.

Another barrier was the registration process, which might have left out particularly critical user groups who did not want to register via email or Facebook Connect. Apart from registration, regular and everyday life communication channels like Facebook are most likely to be used. It was hard to get people away from already existing platforms onto a new platform as nowadays most users can easily debate a topic of their choice on social media platforms, and often prefer to do so.

Gender and other demographic data did not seem to be a problem in online participation in the OurSpace case, and female decision makers seemed to take part more actively in the process and users were equally distributed across the gender category. Cultural conditions might have been an obstacle regarding users participating in discussions in cross-cultural ways, and language has proved a major obstacle in cross-cultural debates despite an integrated translation tool (Google Translate) and many attempts by the consortium to get users from different countries to participate in a discussion. This was most successful for the EU layer; still discussions were mostly in English. Regarding political and cultural conflicts, those were handled well on the platform, and even very different political opinions were handled with a respectful tone making moderation mostly necessary related to process and not tone of discussions.

5   Summary and Conclusion

Summarising, the OurSpace project can be seen as a model for a diverse and politically interested young target group. It was, however, difficult to engage young people beyond the group of politically interested young people. Young users thought that reaching politicians can be a true feature of the platform and they believed that the platform could serve as a link between opinions of the young and decision makers. The content of the platform was seen as highly valuable by all interviewed groups, however, young people wished for more connections between users of the platform. Young people are generally very positive regarding e-participation as a tool for political engagement and informed decision making, even though they are critical about the outcome and they, as a tendency, do not think it can considerably improve trust in politics on a general level. They are critically regarding the political impact on policies and need guidelines when participating in large scale and multi-level e-participation projects on the process level. They are, however, very capable to engage in face-to-face and anti-hierarchal discussions with both politicians and other users, and to engage in respectful and inclusive deliberation online. Engaging decision makers on the platform was one of the major success factors and users expressed their wish to see more politicians on the platform. Getting a commitment from official institutions or decision makers should thus be priority and decision makers should be engaged from as early on as possible in designing e-participation projects. In terms of barriers that prevented users from active discussion, several ones have been depicted, such as: language barriers, higher interest in national rather than European topics and difficulties to navigate on the platform. While users gave positive feedback about the design and functionality of the deliberation process, the ratio of proposals to posts was not satisfying, as users did not come up with their own proposals as often as expected. This might be due to two reasons: The participation threshold for formulating your own solution to a political problem is too high for the average user, or not all users understood the proposal-functionality of the platform. It is thus crucial to promote all stages of the deliberation process and to offer participation opportunities with a lower participation level or threshold, such as liking or thumbing, where users can express their opinion by just promoting comments or proposals with a single click. The same applies to the participation threshold at the registration process: Retrospectively, e-participation, especially in a political context, should not require registration at all levels of participation. As complex discussions can lead to exclusion of less educated and elaborated people the threshold for participation for people who are less familiar with those topics should be kept as low as possible. For any e-participation project with an EU focus this can mean to include as much information on the EU and related processes as possible, as the EU is still an unfamiliar entity in the context of everyday life topics of young people. Additional information can be summarised in blogs, social media channels, or dedicated workshops. Similarly, social features and connectivity is important for users. It is thus advised to create social features users know from other social networking sites and services and to create links to those services (e.g. connection to user profiles, groups, communication possibilities between users, chat functions, thumbing etc.).

References

1. Macintosh, A., Whyte, A.: Towards an evaluation framework for e-participation. Transforming Government: People, Process and Policy 2(1), 16–30 (2008)
2. Sachs, M., Schoßböck, J.: Evaluation of e-participation projects. In: Parycek, P., Edelmann, N. (eds.) CeDEM13. Proceedings of the International Conference for E-Democracy and Open Government, pp. S.465–S.469. Edition Donau-Universität Krems, Krems (2013)
3. Prensky, M.: Digital Natives, Digital Immigrants. On The Horizon. MCB University Press, vol. 9(5) (2001)
4. Coleman, S., Freschi, A.C., Mambrey, P. (eds.): Making e-participation Policy. A European Analysis. [Demo-Net 14.2 and 14.4] (2009), http://www.ssoar.info/ssoar/GetDocument/?resid=6677 (accessed March 27, 2014)
5. Aichholzer, G., Westholm, H.: Evaluating e-participation Projects: Practical Examples and Outline of an Evaluation Framework. European Journal of ePractice (7) (2009), http://www.epractice.eu/files/7.3.pdf (accessed March 27, 2014)

6. Lippa, B. (ed.): D13.3 Demo-Net booklet e-participation Evaluation and Impact (2008), http://www.ifib.de/publikationsdateien/DEMOnet_booklet_13.3_e-participation_evaluation.pdf (accessed March 27, 2014)
7. Medaglia, R.: e-participation Research: A Longitudinal Overview. In: Tambouris, E., Macintosh, A., de Bruijn, H. (eds.) ePart 2011. LNCS, vol. 6847, pp. 99–108. Springer, Heidelberg (2011)
8. Kubicek, H., Lippa, B., Koop, A.: Erfolgreich beteiligt? Nutzen und Erfolgsfaktoren internetgestützter Bürgerbeteiligung – eine empirische Analyse von 12 Fallbeispielen. Bertelsmann, Gütersloh (2011)
9. Wagner, M., Johann, D., Kritzinger, S.: Voting at 16: Turnout and the quality of vote choice. Electoral Studies 31(2), 372–383 (2011)
10. Parycek, P., Diendorfer, G., Maier-Rabler, U., Innen, M., Schossboeck, J., Wirth, M., Neumayer, C.: Internetkompetenz von SchülerInnen. Themeninteressen, Aktivitätsstufen und Rechercheverhalten in der 8. Schulstufe in Österreich. In: Donau-Universität Krems, Studienbericht (2010)
11. Barata, G., Gama, S., Jorge, J., Gonçalves, D.: Improving Participation and Learning with Gamification   (2013),   http://web.ist.utl.pt/gabriel.barata/wp-content/papercite-data/pdf/barata2013c.pdf (accessed March 21, 2014)
12. Newton, K.: Trust, Social Capital, Civil Society, and Democracy. International Political Science Review 22(2), 201–214 (2001)
13. Spescha, P.: Vertrauen in die heimische Politik auf dem Tiefpunkt. In: Wirtschaftsblatt 10.12.2012 (2012),
http://wirtschaftsblatt.at/home/nachrichten/oesterreich/1299460/Vertrauen-in-heimische-Politik-auf-dem-Tiefpunkt
(accessed March 21, 2014)
14. Statista 2014, Europäische Kommission. "Wie sehr vertrauen Sie der österreichischen Regierung?"
http://de.statista.com/statistik/daten/studie/284876/umfrage/umfrage-in-oesterreich-zum-vertrauen-in-die-regierung-2013/
(accessed March 21, 2014).
15. Statista 2014, Europäische Komission. "Welchen Politikern vertrauen Sie am meisten?"
http://de.statista.com/statistik/daten/studie/191776/umfrage/vertrauen-in-politiker/ (accessed March 21, 2014)

Author Index